Spirit Guided Lucid Dreaming

By Nick Barrett

Copyright © 2012 Nick Barrett

Print Edition

ALL RIGHTS RESERVED. This book contains material protected under International and Federal Copyright Laws and Treaties. Any unauthorized reprint or use of this material is prohibited. No part of this book may be reproduced or transmitted in any form or by any means, electronic or mechanical, including photocopying, recording, or by any information storage and retrieval system without express written permission from the author / publisher.

Special Thanks to...

Special thanks to my spirit guide, Clifftoft and the remaining members of my spirit family, for helping me write this book alongside all of the incredible journeys we have all shared together. Without them, none of this information would have ever come into fruition.

A huge thanks to romance novelist, Heather Justesen! You have proved to be a great newfound friend. Thank you for all the support and kindness you've shown and making sure that my book was formatted and edited correctly.

A massive thanks to Paul at 'Create Imaginations', for designing such an incredible front cover! You took an idea and converted it into a reality. Thank you.

Sending all my love and gratitude to my family back in England, and to all of the dedicated readers of my blog, without you, there would be an empty lonely space for me to continue. Your divine inspiration motivates me to higher aspirations everyday.

Lastly, thanks to my partner, Marion. The one, who has really stuck by me from day one! BIG thanks for putting up with all of my weirdness and freaky sleep experiments and never complaining once about it! Always listening to my spirit guided journeys and giving me loving support with my dream studies. I love you dearly...

Table of Contents

Forward

Chapter One - My Guide and I
Meeting my guide

Upon reflection

Use of my spirit's name today

Joining of the two minds

Chapter Two - Observations and Characteristics
Indirect Teachings

Interactions

Sustaining the dream environment

The Sacred Steps

SGLD Stability

Chapter Three - Adapting to SGLD
Power of Thought

The First Stage in SGLD

Adopting the Right SGLD Attitude

Exercise for SGLD Mindset

Training Your Awareness

SGLD Preparation

SGLD Diet

Supplements that Assist Dreaming

My Favourite Dream Herb
SGLD Crystals and Gemstones
Physical Practices
Balancing Exercise

Chapter Four - Dream Journal; Your Gateway to Wisdom
Ideal Dream Journal Features
Occurrences & Objects
Objective Setting

Chapter Five - SGLD Techniques and Traditional methods
Essential Preparations
Traditional Techniques
The MILD Technique
Wake Back to Bed (WBTB)
The DILD Technique
The DEILD Technique
The WILD Technique
Intermittent Timer Technique
SGLD Techniques
SG Hand Mudra
SGLD Meditation
Ideal SGLD Time for Meditation
SGLD Ritual
SGLD Garden
SGLD Exchange Method

SGLD Summoning

SGLD Awakening Method

Chapter Six - Polyphasic Sleep & Dream

Sleep Cycles

Adaptation Period

Time Distortion

My Experience

Reset and Prepare

Chapter Seven - A Helping Hand In Times of Need

Facing your Inner Demons

SGLN Method (Spirit Guided Lucid Nightmare)

The Crow People- SGLN Experience

Upon Reflection

The Hooded Old Lady

Tall Beasts (Crow People)

Chapter Eight - Mirrored Awakenings

My Mirrored Awakening

The Real Meaning of Number Eight

Just When You Least Expect It!

Finding Your Metaphysical Key

Clifftoft Rock

Conclusion

About the Author

Forward

Have you ever considered having a sacred companion who can be beckoned by your call at anytime? Someone that is physically invisible to the naked eye, yet always watching over you? Maybe synchronistic events are starting to occur in your life? Still, you think that it's a strange coincidence! A silent, yet profoundly loud voice speaking directly to your soul, constantly looking out for your best interest...

The very fact that you're reading this unique subject suggests that this voice could have guided you here today! Paradoxically speaking, this voice is already a part of your higher self. The higher self is incredibly wise and has ascended to the celestial domain eons ago. A cosmic guru if you will, that has been evolving for thousands and thousands of years. This voice is, in fact, you and the essence is from an omnipresent source. Although it may appear that its energies could be located outside of your being, this is not the case. The spirit or higher-self part of your spiritual makeup knows you extremely well, overseeing your every thought, action and dream. It is your deepest, innermost feelings along with a complete magnitude of sensory perception, being guided along the way by a loving spirit family.

Every spirit family has a prime passion, which is to guide, nurture and love us, seeing that we grow to reach our spiritual evolution. They have collectively achieved such an alliance since the beginning of time, making sure that humankind is never left alone with just the ego-mind. Patiently, they stand by our sides in a non-intrusive manner, diligently obeying the universal laws and observing us with a non-judgmental eye.

When you and your higher self come together consciously, the connection becomes stronger and unbreakable. Through dreaming lucidly, we too can make that bond with our very own spirit family. Just think, you can now visually meet them all face to face and what a joy it is to know that we're not alone in this universe! Could this be seen as extra-terrestrial communication? Possibly.

They are metaphysical in nature and can enter our dreams anytime. They can morph and transmute themselves as they wish, whilst simultaneously blending into our unique dreamscapes. Multidimensional beings that hop from one place to the next!

How can we be sure that this is not just a figment of our imaginations? Well, my philosophy is that the whole universe is built on imagination and imagination comes from thoughts. So if we can surely think it then it can become a reality! We attract what we desire in life from the energy we put in. So the first step is shifting our awareness and energies in truly understanding how crucial spirit guides are. We must believe, not just with our minds but also with our hearts.

A few years ago I felt compelled to seek out my own spirit guide. I did not know any particular way or technique in doing so, but was already accustomed to lucid dreaming. So this seemed to be the best option for me. I knew that there was something more, something that felt bigger within myself that desperately needed discovering. Today I have an incredibly strong connection with my guide who is truly my best friend. I have asked him to guide me whilst writing this book, so that all the information contained can assist others with the necessary tools to help them in their own quest. Above all, to inspire and seek forth their own spirit family. I will go into great detail about my guide in the chapter named 'My Guide and I'.

If you are thinking to yourself, this cannot be possible and this sounds extremely unfathomable, then you may wish to see scientific proof! Unfortunately, spirit guides cannot simply go onto television and prove their existence at this time. But they will most certainly make themselves known to us individually within our multi-sensory attunement, just as we are willing to show ourselves to them.

Consider this next notion, 'something that cannot be seen in the physical world does not necessarily mean it does not exist.'

Inter-dimensional worlds, over-laced into the next, coexisting simultaneously whilst regulating at different energetic frequencies, could be the next breakthrough in tomorrow's mainstream science. But, until then we must look deep within ourselves for the answers we seek. Intuitive knowing and feeling is paramount when sealing this sacred bond between you and spirit. It is not simply lying in your bed and waiting for your next lucid adventure. It is a full-time state of being. We must expand our higher energetic awareness so that we can attract the harmonic frequency of the angelic realm.

The research I have gathered, including excerpts from my dream journal, has all been documented into its clearest form possible so that there will be no risk of confusion. My spirit guided lucid experiences will be scattered throughout, depending on the topic at hand. This will benefit you in understanding the true teachings and symbolic nature of my guide's message.

Here you will find your unique centre in becoming more attuned to the 'spirit frequency' that is required when contacting your guide through dreaming. Adopting the correct psychology for this practice is absolute. Having the correct state of mind is a foundational start. I'll go into further detail in the chapter named 'Adaptation to SGLD'. Please note that when you see the abbreviation 'SGLD', this means 'Spirit Guided Lucid Dreaming', which is used numerous times throughout the course of this read.

The aim of this book is to find a 'loop-hole' in inter-dimensional companionship through dreaming. The goal of my research is to shed new light and discover fresh ideals and comparisons in the field of SGLD.

Included are traditional techniques for lucid dreaming and advanced SGLD techniques that will benefit the dreamer. It is my suggestion that if you're new to lucid dreaming, you should first study the traditional techniques for at least a few months, achieving multiple successful lucid adventures, then moving onto to SGLD techniques afterwards. Failure to do so will impede and confuse your progress. To accompany those techniques, I have also incorporated the ideal SGLD diet, alternate sleep cycles and meditational exercises. One should consider amplifying and attuning their energetic field to make spirit contact. Harmonising the mind, body and spirit principle supports the dreamer. This will ensure the dreamer builds a healthy and correct foundation into SGLD.

I come before you, humbly with only my research and experiences, which is all I can offer. I propose, that each and every one of us, are all teachers and have distinct diverse expressions created from the same infinite source. We can all learn a great deal from each other and ourselves. It is only right that I share this phenomenon with you, no matter how unexplainable and surreal it may seem to the common man. I wish to, at the very least, in-spire you so that you too can be in-spirit...

I have no doubt that you will be successful on your spirit-guided journey through lucid dreaming.

Do we have to be spiritual to have a spirit guide?

Growing up, from a very religious background, I soon discovered that the beliefs I had been taught didn't add up for me. I always felt a deep connection from the cosmos, and that there was a superior intelligence. What exactly that was, I did not know. All I had were the old Bible stories my parents used to read me.

The question of whether or not religion is a good or bad thing and which faith is the best, has been a mundane conundrum for thousands of years.

Today I feel that all religions, with their teachings, have some truth and similarities to each other. It is the interpretation and perception that has gotten lost in translation. They all speak of chains of events in the same order, which could be deemed as "similar." One particular faith therefore is speaking about the next and so on. I will not list details of these religious events. These similar perspectives are looked at from scholars and bible historians across the planet. They are all beginning to realise the distinct similarities shared by each faith that cannot be ignored, and to simply shove it under the carpet, so to speak.

Having said that, whatever your belief system, it is of course, entirely up to you. I do not wish to impede on anyone's faith, nor question the religious ground they stand upon.

Instead, I propose being simply open to the universe. This is not a belief system, telling you how you should think and feel. People today get confused greatly with the terminology "Spiritual." The true ignorance of this terminology is them thinking that you are religious or from a new-age cult. This is not the case. Nor is it a belief system. It just is. Being spiritual does not require a Bible or even a particular God to worship. Like accepting infinite space and consciousness, it is a state of being. Not being placed into any particular bracket of conformity.

When you move to a place of simply being, you begin to tear down the illusory veil of what man has created. Man cannot design and build a divinely intelligent, universal spiritual system alone. You now shift your perspective to a place of peace, love and harmony and you will begin to notice and feel the energies of the endless universe, learning to cultivate this essence inwardly and outwardly.

Thousands of years ago, among many other esoteric civilisations, the ancient Chinese studied the divine nature of the universe. Predominantly, they learned to cultivate life-force energy or Qi (pronounced 'chee'). They understood the distinct correlation between the vast universe and the human body. By being in harmony with the flow of the universal Qi and cultivating its magic within the body, they were never prone to disease, and health ailments were restored back to normal.

Advanced practitioners of cultivating Qi from ancient China, evolved to being ascended masters, living as immortals with super-human capabilities. They discovered that the universe shared the same reflective nature as our physical bodies because every living molecule is made up of energy. Essentially Qi is the life force of life. Through the energetic pathways of the body, also known as meridians, they could determine where the life-force energy was most abundant. If there was a problem within the body, they would energetically balance this using their connection to the cosmos to guide them. When the energy becomes stagnant and eventually diminishes, like when we age, so will certain areas of the body, which then leads to disease or death.

That's why it's important for us to connect as much as possible to the life-force energy and be in tune with the universe, so we too, can cultivate our own powerful force, by always keeping the Qi circulated. There is an abundant amount of divine energy available to us all. When we consciously re-connect ourselves to the primordial source, immeasurable celestial help begins to reopen us to ourselves.

Quantum physicists are now beginning to understand this notion, which the ancient Taoists knew thousands of years ago. The ancient knowledge however, does not have to be lost in translation this time around. When we decide to look within ourselves, our divine birthright is now redeemed. No further studying is needed when making this connection. This very essence is within you right now. That's really what being spiritual is about. Learning to look within, removing any self-created barriers and connecting once again with the universal energies to expand your consciousness.

I don't believe that there is only one way to receive guidance from a spirit. I feel, no matter what religious or spiritual background you may have, as long as you're open with a non-judgmental attitude and acting from a place of unconditional love, you will be sure to receive all the guidance available. The universal energies do not judge nor single out any minority, all it knows and is ever capable of, is simply to love. Like each and every one of us, this is the place that all spirit guides come from, the source. So when we are finally living from the heart-center, by choosing to love instead of hate, we will attract more happiness into our lives.

Today's View on Dreaming

Most children who are sensitive to the energies at an early age are frightened and confused. This is sad because they have not been fully taught the importance of dreaming and the powers of the mind. If we were to remain in a state of innocence and retain this way of using the mind, there probably would be no war today.

As humans, we fear what we do not understand. At times we can be ignorant and claim to already know everything, utilising only the (well-known) five normal senses. This creates psychological barriers and the mind can only go so far, thus obstructing our ability to delve deeper into the subconscious part of ourselves. In today's Western society through religion, media, politics and institutionalised educational systems, we are steered away from looking at the unseen, metaphysical energies that are in and around us.

Unfortunately, the Western culture is more directed towards thinking with their heads and not from their hearts. Understanding our divine nature on a much deeper level through practices such as meditation and conscious dreaming, is classed as uncommon and strange. However, I believe that this view is changing for the better. The teachings of Tibetan Dream Yoga and other ancient dream teachings are now more and more accessible to modern Western society. The East has truly moved to the West, and now we can all enjoy the fruits of our ancestral teachings.

Lucid dreaming, astral travel, out-of-body experiences, soul travel and many more, are all states of high awareness. A view on how we label those many types of lucidity regularly gets misconstrued within the dreaming community. Everyone has his or her own unique interpretation and view when experiencing this phenomenon. If I'm asked, "what should I call this state?" I will always refer the question back as to why the practitioner wishes to label and define the experience in the first place.

Of course there are lucid methodologies which have names, but the actual experience itself, is not so definable. Like the universe being an infinite space, so is the infinite capability of consciousness with endless possibilities. What we define as a whole should not be our prime focus here. Someone else's experience and perception will most certainly be different in nature to mine or the next person's. Everyone on planet Earth has infinite amounts of the universal expression. That's what makes us all so intelligently diverse. How creative the universal mind truly is!

However, through a state of sleep paralysis (sleep/awaken state combined), we tend to experience bodily sensations such as strong vibrations rushing through the body, hearing gusty sounds like heavy wind being blown into our ear drums and having a feeling as though we're a heavy lead weight etc. All of these sensations, and many others, are common for this kind of sleeping state. In a sense, these paralysis symptoms are a way in sharing with each other. A great sense of comfort hits us when we realise others are experiencing the same. Why is this though? To prove that we're not actually turning crazy? Not at all, far from it. Subconsciously, we know that we are all connected to each other in some way. So when others feel what we feel, it makes things a little less daunting for us.

The layering of conscious dreaming can be subtle and it can be difficult to recognise the slight differences when in either the awake or sleeping state.

Instead, the dreamer grows along his or her journey of self-discovery. The focus now shifts off the conundrum of trying to 'label the experience' and now moves more towards expanding ones own spiritual consciousness, having dedicated a purpose to finding a deeper meaning to the sacred art of dreaming.

My Guide & I

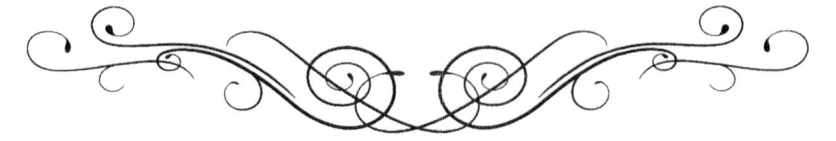

Chapter One

As a child, I was always intuitively sensitive to the other forces. Growing up from age five years and up, I began to draw in certain characteristics that are mostly common in young children today. I distinctly remember seeing flashing orbs around my bed on many nights and hearing unseen voices, a feeling of someone quickly tickling the back of my neck as I lay on my side. I would observe and be in a state of shock, my heart would thump as hard as it could whilst being in a moment of utter confusion. If I were ever scared and alone, I would always feel that I was in the company of an invisible mystic presence that can be described as a "caring ghost-type of being." This was a regular occurrence for me, no matter how bizarre it may have seemed. But, deep down, I always knew that this thing would make itself known to me one day.

As I matured, so did my senses. I could see spirits and feel unexplainable energies that were not from this space and time. Growing up, I specifically remember living with my family in a 16th - century house that was very spooky. Local villages recited old ghost stories about that house and claimed to have had spirit-like encounters, seeing something ghostly dashing past our living room windows. The feeling of strange vibes lurking around the nooks and crannies were more than obvious. Floors creaked, window sills whistled and a feeling of being watched was omnipresent.

Most of my family claimed to have felt something in that house at one time or another. I had many unexplainable encounters during my childhood years there. From time to time when I dream, I still visit this house. It's quite possible that my subconscious mind is notifying me to unlock a past childhood memory.

I also received regular prophetic dreams that had shaped my consciousness and belief system to what it is today. This certainly stoked my curiosity. leading me to discovering the true magnificence of alternate states of consciousness, including lucid dreaming.

My lucid dream adventures really hit a peak point during the 2008 global economy crisis. Many people, including myself, were made redundant. I had been working for a major electronics company based in Central London for four years. Just like that, I had to leave with no reconcile payment due to the company downsizing!

This made a huge impact to my professional and social life. Money was scarce and I needed to find a new emotional release to combat the stress I was experiencing. My body was suffering in the process and as a result, some of my hair started to fall out. The homestead was financially on shaky ground and my relationship with my partner was under immense pressure.

For the next two years, I used my time to search and apply for jobs, but still had no real progress. Major personal budgeting was put into place because the government credit was never enough. I regularly had to go without food. Job opportunities were few and the competition was even greater than before. These were dark times for everyone, I'm sure you'll agree!

However, despite my depressing environment and lack of occupation, I discovered that all of the answers I ever sought had been staring at me the whole time. Through focusing on my dreams and understanding my higher self's message, I could overcome any obstacle that my life threw at me! This was now my primary focus. Besides, it was all I had left!

So I meditated day and night using unique mantras, significant only to my dream studies. I changed my diet into a complete vegetable and fruit diet and cancelled all refined processed foods and dairy. Fasting and detoxifying my body was my new disciplined routine. I drank lots of fresh water from natural springs and replaced caffeine with green tea. I cut out all of the external distractions like television, radio and newspapers etc. Selling my television was the best decision I ever made! Reading and researching the fascinating world of dreams was so much more enjoyable.

I took longs walks out into nature not knowing where the trail ended and connected to Mother Earth's beauty. Old friendships and acquaintances that were not in accordance to my higher self gradually diminished. I documented my dream entries daily, as soon as the dream ended that night, lucid or not, I'd awaken myself naturally, turn on my pocket torch and write down all that occurred, making sure that I didn't miss one single detail. I set my intention to be lucid, incubated my dream goals and meditated on them. I hoped that one day something, or someone, could bring me closer to understanding. What that thing was exactly, I had no idea.

I then started to feel that familiar, forgotten presence again, like an old friend that I hadn't seen for many years. So, curiously, within my dream world, I'd commonly ask dream characters their purpose and where they came from. Trying to understand how, when and why, whilst documenting and analysing all my recorded dream entries. Trusting my "gut feeling" was now at the forefront of my practice. I distinctly remember one particular lucid dream that was an important turning point in my newfound direction;

I am at a conference and I appear to be the guest speaker. There must be approximately one hundred people watching me right now. I feel confident about the talk. I'm completely aware that I'm dreaming and I quickly remember my intention, 'to seek out and discover any possible spirits that may be watching over me'. I immediately raise my voice and yell,

"Can I please see a show of hands who are projected from my subconscious mind?"

To my surprise, over half of them put their hands up instantly. I now ponder and wonder, who are the remaining ones who didn't raise their hands? I now walk over to a few of them sitting on the front row.

I ask a young, dark haired woman, "Who are you?"

She replies, "We are your friends, Nick, and always will be".

Surprisingly they all look extremely familiar to me, even though I have never met them before! It feels like I know them all somehow. I can sense her consciousness in some way and I suspect she can sense mine. Why do I feel so safe around them, and not know them at all?

Strange and unexplainable lucid dreams continued as the months progressed. I kept using the same formula in deciphering the spirits from the subconscious projections. One could argue that spirits are made up entirely from our subconscious mind. But, I believe they differ considerably in nature and I will explain this comparison in great detail further along.

I began to develop a new sense of precognitive awareness; the spirit's energies would present themselves to me as I entered the lucid dream. I experienced more lucidity and the spirit energies were now being attracted in vast quantities to the energy I was inputting into my dreams. It was almost like it was mirroring what I originally initiated.

It was something I had to practice, but with time I got stronger and more attuned to its specific metaphysical blueprint. Even if the spirit was disguised as a different dream character, gender or playing a certain role within a storyboard, I could still sense when it were observing me. I'd simply stop, point and say,

"Hey, I know it's you! Uncloak yourself immediately, so that I can truly see who you are!"

Then the being would morph into its true self. A spirit that was uniquely familiar to me alone.

Even though I could trace the spirit's unique energy pattern, it was extremely difficult for me to remember the characteristics of the face. Upon awakening, I would sketch out possible portraits of the spirit's face (to the best of my novice drawing skills that is!) This proved to be somewhat challenging.

Another interesting fact that was fairly common during the beginning: as I got close to the spirit's face, my full peripheral was then filled with a panoramic view of his/her face. The eyes told a thousand stories; they appeared to be incredibly wise and ancient. The more I tried to focus upon the face, the more it morphed into different features. A sensation of vertigo crept over me the more I tried to adjust my dream-eyes and focus. Just like a blip within the spectrum of light.

Another way to describe this characteristic is like when an old computer monitor changed pictures. The image flickered rapidly. One identity, including clothing, can be morphed and replaced with another instantaneously. It was difficult for me to not get distracted when conversing with the spirit. Today, I have no problem with this and the flickering visuals seem to have settled. Maybe, my dream-self has become more accustomed to a particular frequency that matches the spirits'.

I began to keep my dream journal close to me, even more now. I took it everywhere I went, safely secure in the back pocket of my trousers. I was constantly reading past entries for further insights that were astonishingly boundless in time. It was truly a personal gateway to the other side and physical proof of my guided adventures. A magical journal indeed! I found that by being ultimately disciplined, in the pursuit of decoding my dreams, using personal time to reflect upon its wording brought me to higher wisdom of self-discovery.

It was evident now, that a loving spirit family was guiding me through my dreams and waking life. Mirroring worlds reflecting upon each other, and I was located within the borderlands. Signs of symbology manifesting from the waking and dreaming reality. The questions in my mind still arouse thoughts such as, who were my spirit family? Where did they come from? What are their names?

My first real breakthrough in SGLD began when I went to live in India for six months. I stayed in a beautiful community called, AuroVille, just outside of Pondicherry, southern India. I remember on the plane during take off, meditating to myself, hoping to make an official connection with my spirit family. My intention was strong and my mission was set into place.

In this community I purchased a beautiful new dream journal made from only natural materials that was beautifully handmade by the local villages. I meditated regularly in the 'Matrimandir' temple, a megalithic golden dome covered in twenty-eight-karat gold leaf with a huge crystal ball located in its center. Heightening my awareness and intention even more. Connecting to the source. The feeling of a spirit companion sitting right next to me, as I sat crossed legged, concentrating with my hands clasped.

Meeting my Guide

My dreams began to take on a whole new shape, old and forgotten issues of my past were now surfacing and a great healing was at hand. Lucid dreams were extremely vibrant and real. My consciousness was being transported to other alien worlds, something that I thought was not possible. Full clarity and definition, immersed my (dream) body. Out-of-body experiences, also known as "astral projection," began to manifest spontaneously as I went to sleep. I remember being awoken by strange screeching sounds ringing in my ears and the sensation of my whole physical body vibrating at an incredible rate.

Then came a dream, which would change my life forever...

I see a door up ahead and it's full of many different colours! I walk through and wonder what's on the other side? I appear on the other side, it looks like an old fishing town and the sun is shining. I feel happy and at peace. I look at my hands and realise that I'm lucid! I say, "Hey! My hands look all funny and cartoony, how strange!" I'm firmly grounded into the dreamscape. I walk into the town's center to find a big clock tower overlooking many people walking. They seem to be occupied with their business. I see some other people on bicycles too. I remember my usual 'shout-out routine',

"SPIRIT GUIDE! SPIRIT GUIDE!"

I sigh and wait patiently, anticipating a reaction from something or someone.

Suddenly an old man whizzes past me on a bicycle whilst jingling the bell to get my attention.

"Hey you, wait!" I say telepathically.

He comes to an immediate stop, still facing away from me.

"Please come back, I want to speak to you!" I yell over to the old stranger.

He turns round and peddles back to me. We sit on a bench together.

"Are you my spirit guide?"

"Yes," he replies telepathically with a long smile

"Is there any more of you?" I excitedly ask like a kid in a candy shop.

"Now, is not the right time for you to know this, much bigger things are at stake."

The feeling of joy filled my bloodstream, hearing his audible attentive voice for the first time.

"I met you before, right? In my other dreams?" I ask.

The old man's face looks at me with admiration for my cunning perceptiveness.

"Yes," He replies, firmly stating the obvious.

"eh...I need your help."

The spirit's eyes gleam with what was already foreseen. "You do not need my help, Nick."

A feeling of trust radiates out from the old man's gentle voice.

"Can you hear my thoughts spirit?" I say telepathically.

"Yes, it sounds like sh-shs-shhhhhhsh," he said aloud, whilst joking.

The old man's sense of humor is displayed whilst imitating a static radio signal. We both laugh and agree that this has "some" truth.

The dream fades...

Upon Reflection

After this first real encounter with my spirit guide, I finally felt I had the proof that I was searching for. I woke up with an ecstatic feeling of joy! It was like I just uncovered the universes most treasured secret and I accomplished all this through lucid dreaming. I finally made metaphysical contact from which I had felt was shaping my consciousness all along. Completely motivated to go deeper into the unknown, I ventured even further into understanding my new spirit friend.

Throughout this SGLD experience, I'm mainly connecting with one of the main members of the spirit family. The chosen name that I'm given at this time is, Clifftoft. To the collective, this name/label is irrelevant, they use higher states of consciousness to communicate with each other alongside many other hidden talents. The label system they have in place for humans is for our understanding and comprehension. We tend to understand things more clearly and with ease when we can name/label something. As humans we can comprehend a lot more efficiently when we are able to adopt names to things we physically see which coincide with our linear 3D terminology.

Whilst in India, I drew a very rough sketch of Clifftoft (fig.1). He appeared frequently in this similar style during the early stages of our lucid relationship. But since then, over the years he has changed into many genders, ages, styles and forms.

Figure 1 Rough sketch of Clifftoft

I came about this interesting spirit name during an extremely vivid astral projection. It was all set in a colossal-sized space station to which Clifftoft had taken me. I seemed to be there for what felt like about five earth hours. During my visit, I was greeted by a group of extra-tall human-like beings wearing tight space outfits that were sleek and slender. They appeared to be at least three-times taller than my actual height, and I'm six feet tall! Chrome walls surrounded me, circular electronic control panels that were all built into the interior of the station. There were magnificent views out into deep space as I peered through the megalithic glass-viewing screen.

Clifftoft is in front of me, escorting me to all of the scheduled meeting points. I instinctively felt compelled to request a contact name for the spirit that was hosting the show. I ask that his name be displayed on a huge electronic panel with red digital lettering. This was because I couldn't hear at first, and I wanted to get the spelling just right. I remember one particular conversation with one of the female space cadets who I now know to be from my spirit family. I asked her, "How would I summon you, if I needed to get hold of you?" She replied,

"It is only a human need, not our need, but here is a name you may use..."

This intrigued me and empowered my inquisitiveness even more. The name flashed on the panel and I made extra effort to remember its unique letter formation by repeatedly saying it aloud to myself, "C.....L......I......F......F......T.....O......F......T."

First seeing it on the electronic metal board was incredibly strange and elaborate. They can manifest any object at will, I thought to myself.

From then on I was asked a series of questions by a panel of five humanoids. A galactic spirit-council in some way. I won't go into detail exactly what they asked me, since this is personal information to my guiding family and I. However, I will mention that I was most incredibly put to the test. At times, they questioned my darkest fears, unmasking long-forgotten personality traits that needed to be brought to light. It felt like I was being mentally challenged within a soul-personality-testing suite!

Feeling a little woozy after that encounter, I then got chaperoned to the next test, they told me to sit within this sound booth. They played a selection of songs that was fictitiously sung by me and I had never heard them before! Being already accustomed to music in the past, singing on tracks seemed only familiar to me. Maybe they were demonstrated in such a way to trigger certain characteristics within my subconscious later? Looking back, I believe this to be a healing centre for the mind, uncovering hidden truths and healing emotional wounds from the past.

My final test was for them to understand what level of psychic ability I already acquired during my time on earth and in this life. I was sent to an enormous circular metal platform, which was placed in the middle of a space hangar. Within the walls were small square screens that gave off a yellow glow when focused upon. A tall, bearded man greeted me on this platform; I believe this to be my guide. He pointed to one of the many squares on the ship's interior. There must be millions of them! Far too many to count! He gets me to guess which one will glow next. I point to the first one that I focus upon; it then glows brightly in the distance. Seconds after this, the correct panel glows below. Although I was a few rows out, I thought that this was not a bad result to say it's my first try! I was pretty pleased with myself. My guide and I played this entertaining game for quite some time and I seemed to become more advanced the more I played. This test seemed to upgrade my existing intuitive self even further.

Use of my Spirit's name today

I use this name today for beckoning my spirit guide. I suspect that other dreamers can do the same once their spirit-bond is sealed when the correct awareness is adopted. Summoning spirits come in a variety of other forms, such as, channeling, meditation, tarot and séances. People all around the world connect with other beings from another space and time, who can be called upon at any time with their chosen name.

Joining of the two minds

Through the years, Clifftoft and I have built a respectful loving relationship outside and inside the dream world. He has become my best friend, my advisor, my (dream) shoulder to cry on when I need comforting, my metaphysical mirror and my very own genie if I had a wish that needed granting. He is I and I am he. My life now feels complete because I have sealed the divine bond.

During an SGLD exchange, (later I will discuss what that is exactly) I asked him to show me an example of how we were both interlinked in the universe.

During the beginning stages of my SGLD development, it was all about why and how, so that my linear demons could comprehend what was actually happening.

That very night he kindly sent me a dream in which I became spontaneously lucid.

We meet in an old medieval tavern. The place is packed full of different sorts of people and beer and music is abundant. I notice him sitting at a table accompanied by the rest of my spirit family. He is easy to spot because of his red leather jacket. He beckons me over; I greet him and the others. I am really pleased to see him as it has been over a week since we last met. I throw my arms around him and we hug each other.

In that moment, I notice where we are standing. Facing me is a large mirror and he has his back to it. Whilst still hugging, I'm looking at our reflection, only to find something really incredible! At first, I expect to see my reflection and think everything is normal, but I could have been mistaken. Instead, I find his reflection looking straight back at me! But how is this so?

He just smiles back at me in the mirror. Holding one another, I notice this even more because I see us both wearing red jackets in the reflection. He manifested an optical illusion for my eyes only. I suddenly feel a telepathic wave overcome me, that this is a demonstration in how our two minds were interlinked. A unique fusion of a divine soul unification. One soul, one mind.

From that point on, I never questioned again what my spirit guide was to me. Through the mirrored reflection of our minds linked together, I began to build on this and become ever more in tune with his (my) vibration. I propose, together we create a new harmonic vibration once the two frequencies are completely in sync with each other, harmoniously working as one. Through asking my spirit guide, he kindly helped me understand this on a much deeper level.

Observations and Characteristics

Chapter Two

Throughout my lucid adventures, I have gathered many observations and characteristics that my spirit guide reveals. Whether or not these behavioral qualities are universal, I'm not certain. Maybe they have adapted themselves to fit our subconscious minds specifically to facilitate us to feel more at ease.

Humorous, witty comments are part of my relationship with my guide. We've also had our serious moments too, but it's always important to remember to enjoy our dream experiences and take into account our inner child. His method in teaching has at times left me wondering. My guide's particular style, if I had to sum up in one word, would be "indirect." This way in teaching me leaves me asking sometimes, why would he say that? Why did he do that just then? No matter how strange, I found that he had a method to his madness, so to speak!

I came to the conclusion that my spirit guide teaches me in this way because the human brain will ask for more, to right itself, to grow on its own accord, instinctually depending on the right influences. If we question something, then we have the drive and curiosity to find out why. It is curiosity that makes our conscious intelligence grow.

However, if my guide simply gave me all the wisdom in the universe quicker than the speed of light, with no time for me to seek out the answer myself, I would not be truly learning and experiencing anything. I would not fully grasp the concept of my guide's message. We have to experience it in order to learn from a situation, good or bad.

Indirect Teachings

For many years, especially during my early youth when I was a musician, I had a problem with self-acceptance. Low self-esteem became a barrier and I thought way too much of what others may (or may not) be thinking. This demon within me affected my relationships, my career and my close friendships. I had to do something about this. But as I got older, I kept on pushing this inner problem to the back, burying it deep within me. I locked it up and pretended it never existed. I was wrong to do this.

Then I met my spirit guide. All of my inner fears and demons came to the surface and showed themselves to me.

Through a SGLD experience, I first saw my guide's indirect methodology.

In the dream, I appear in a small room. I'm immediately standing in front of Clifftoft. His face blankly stares back at mine. I say, "Hey, man, it's you!" I reach out my arm to meet his in a handshake, but he shoves my body away with force!

I lose balance and try to regain my stance. I ask, "Hey, why did you just do that?"

He ignores me.

I try to get close one more time. He shoves me again, this time with more force. I feel disappointed and shocked. Feeling confused, I pull myself out of the SGLD by intent and return back to my earthly bed.

Upon awakening, I think to myself, why would he do this? This is completely out of character. Is he angry with me? What did I do wrong? My thoughts raced, trying to make sense of it all. I felt upset that I might have made my guide unhappy with me. I really didn't want this to be the case, as things were great between us. We were making real progress!

I recall, previously to the SGLD, setting my intention to uncover the hidden demons within that I long forgot. Through meditating on the intention and playing the lucid dream over and over again in my mind, I suddenly realised what my guide was trying to teach me.

He knew all along that shoving me like that, when all I was expecting was a nice meet and greet, would make me question the relationship, feel rejected and think I offended him in some way. He uncovered a hidden aspect of myself that I buried a long time ago. He foresaw how I would react afterwards from the thought processes I experienced upon awakening. He indirectly demonstrated a representation of this fear to me in a lucid dream. The way he structured the dream and saw how it affected me afterwards, proves that our guides know us better than we sometimes know ourselves! As soon as I worked this out, I fully understood the meaning of the message and because of it, healed myself completely of this old demon.

It's important to note, that my guide has not shown me any aggressive shoving since the learning of this very important lesson. Good thing too!

Interactions

The subconscious mind will manifest any thoughts or emotional concerns that we may have and project them in the form of symbolic imagery. Dream objects and landscapes then manifest before our eyes, we then interact with these projections and integrate them with past memories. This can all serve as a great tool for the spirit guide to observe what you are really thinking within the dream world.

I've come to the conclusion that once we are open to our spirit energy, this sequentially acts as an energetic magnet to our own specific energy field. In short, if we are open to meeting our guides, then our guides will find it easier to connect with us. How strong we set our intention will have a dramatic impact on what we wish to attract. Once the bond with spirit is sealed, the remaining spirit family members will come to you in some shape or form. All we have to do is set our minds to receiving the celestial support. Just ask!

Within the dreamscape, stating just a few attributes, spirit guides can add objects, morph into the scenery and revamp features onto your dream body that are in harmony of the subconscious mind. Of course the subconscious mind may at times become a nuisance and get in the way when you and your guide are privately talking, a firm "go away!" from your spirit guide is normal!

I remember in a lucid dream, I felt my guide's presence surrounding me, I called out to him and felt compelled to then investigate the interior of a nearby bar. I walked down the bar to the end, asking projections along the way if they had seen him, or more importantly if it was my guide disguised! Through interrogating six projections, I finally found him sat at a nearby table, he shouts "Nick! Over here!" He sat with other familiar spirits that I have met in other dreams. I sat down and greeted them all telepathically. Then a random female projection (from my subconscious) came to our table and interrupted the conversation. She, my subconscious, felt a little neglected that me (my conscious-self) was giving my spirit guide family the most attention within my dream. Clifftoft then stood up and told her firmly to leave. She got the message, walked away and disappeared. Upon reflection of this lucid dream, I came to the conclusion that my guide has more command over my subconscious than I originally perceived.

Another example of the direct intervention between spirit and my subconscious mind, dramatically made me question the very basis of the two distinctions.

In the lucid dream, I was walking with him within a beautiful scenic village on a glorious sunny day. During this time in waking life I was learning to speak French. My lessons were becoming tiresome and I had little faith that I could ever speak such a language. I was losing my courage to keep trying.

My spirit guide knew that this was becoming a big concern for me before I even mentioned anything to him.

As we walked further along the cobble path talking about mundane things, he briefly stops midsentence, turns round to my face directly and starts spluttering random French words! I was startled by this instant change of sound and had no idea what was being said. My girlfriend (a subconscious projected dream copy) was walking along side me at the same time and then they both walked further along in front of me. I stood there and decided to observe their conversation. It sounds a little heated, I thought to myself! Why was my guide talking to her?

"It is a difficult language, and will take time for him to learn!" My partner says loudly.

"Yes, I understand that, but he has to really want it, he has to really want to learn French in order for him to eventually speak it!" My spirit guide replies firmly.

Upon awakening from the lucid dream, dazed and confused, I wondered what all this really meant. What was this dream's message? Later that day, I reflected upon my dream journal from this unique encounter.

I came to the conclusion that he was also guiding my subconscious part of me face to face in the form of my partner (who was a subconscious manifestation). Thus helping me breakdown any language complex I had with learning French. It all seemed to make sense now; all of my lucid adventures were configured and guided to accomplish my best interest. Even if it meant him talking/influencing directly to my subconscious self! I then began to learn the French language with ease and without my previous hesitation. My complex seemed to vanish thereafter.

Although the subconscious projections of ourselves intervene at times, the spirit family will use it to their advantage and always for the greater good. I remember speaking to Clifftoft in a lucid dream about not having enough time with a certain project and that times were getting a little bit stressful. He asked if I felt a little trapped and scared about this particular thought.

The lucid dream, to my surprise was already a little menacing and began to darken even more. The subconscious projections began to form zombie-like men and women and so started to crowd around us both closely with arms outstretched.

I ignored what surrounded us, I felt completely safe and secure that my guide was present. My spirit guide's eyes drifted off me slightly in mid-conversation and observed the projections as they fearlessly approached. He understood before I knew, that I felt emotionally trapped and under a lot of pressure. He was registering and decoding my dream symbols before I even had chance too! He gained a deeper understanding of the involuntary part of myself.

Even if you make contact with your guide, the subconscious part of you will carry on as normal, no matter how extreme the symbology may seem. You can either interact with it or submerge out of it. The spirit guide's ethos is to be in harmony with the subconscious and essentially put it to good use, as long as it coincides with teaching you the lesson you are supposed to learn at that time.

Sometimes a guide would have to suddenly switch its locality and then fit itself with your subconscious. Even by changing his or hers complete appearance! The guide will adjust and merge, but will always lead you to the next stage in your divine evolution. This relationship with your guide is how we truly get to understand SGLD. Knowing what to look out for and how to employ it to our advantage is crucial.

Sustaining the Dream Environment

Being lucid, when you first realise that you are dreaming, can make the dreamer ecstatic. A fantastic sense of achievement and energy surges all the way through you. You smile and jump for joy that you managed to gain such a mystical awareness! You shout, "Alright! I'm lucid, whoo- hoo!"

This can be a distracting moment at times if you're not use to this achievement. The more we become lucid in our dreams, the more comfortable you feel in this new state of higher awareness. The serious dreamer who wishes to expand and stabilise the environment even greater, can implement a core grounding system that will complement their dreamtime.

Before I share my divine grounding method, it's important to state the most traditional ways in dream stability. Sometimes the simpler things can be just as effective.

Once lucid, you may start with paying particular attention to your breath. Look around you and your dreamscape with deep inquisitiveness. Remain calm and relax your body. Look at your hands now and rub them vigorously. Keep moving at a steady pace whilst stating to yourself that you are in a dream. The intention is to keep the presence of your mind coherent and consistent. Be alert to not get 're-dazed' back into the dream-script as this can trick you if you're not careful.

Engage and intensify all of your known (dream) senses; taste, touch, hearing, sight and smell. Focus upon an object, maybe a leaf from a nearby branch perhaps? Now magnify this with your mind and push your focus all the way through to a microscopic level. You will start to see the image and dreamscape much more crisp and alive now, a complete upgrade compared to your normal surroundings. Demanding out loud, "Clarity Now" can work incredibly well. In fact, you can influence just about anything by requesting aloud. Discover what you and your subconscious can co-create together with affirmations. Remember there are no limits, only the limits we set ourselves internally.

The Sacred Steps

In my early lucid adventures I tried many of the conventional methods in grounding one's environment. This worked well, but I then felt obliged to deepen my efforts and show appreciation. So I created a system of steps to include when first becoming lucid; they have now become a customary routine of my personal grounding method and have brought me a deeper awareness because of it.

Method

You first become aware that you are in a dream, then look at your entire dream body from the ground up, touch the fabric of your clothes and feel your face followed by rubbing your hands. Now, begin walking at a steady pace and put your hands, palms together, as if you were praying. Don't worry, you do not have to be religious for this to work. This will improve concentration.

Keep your palms together whilst walking and interact with the projections that surround you. Greet them and show appreciation to them. Say out loud, "Hello! Thank you so much for allowing me to share this time with you." Show kindness towards them and your environment.

Now look to the ground beneath your feet. Study its textures and composition. Touch and feel the ground with your fingertips and thank the ground you walk upon. Show appreciation to your dreamscape. You will now notice the environment around you becoming more solid and colours begin to appear more vibrant. These steps have maximised the potential of my lucid experiences. The length of the lucid dream will vary depending on how deeply you connect with your environment.

I have had what felt like three-hour adventures by using these sacred steps at the start. It seems to unify you and your subconscious on a much deeper level. A mutual respect is unified between your conscious and subconscious. Instead of being against the current and too emotionally driven, you are more relaxed, calm and harmonious within your dream environment. A great sense of wellbeing will surround you deeper into the experience. Whether you're spiritual or not, I believe this to be a wonderful gift for the long journey ahead.

When I was travelling in India, I hosted a small beginners workshop in lucid dreaming to a group of about thirty people. Most of them had heard about lucid dreaming before and a handful of them experienced a type of lucidity one time or another. I spoke about the sacred steps and I physically demonstrated for them the best way I could. Some group members got back to me after the workshop and claimed to have had successful results. By using this method, it seemed to have strengthened their grounding and overall practice by far.

SGLD Stability

This has to be one of my discovered favourites in gaining greater dream stability from a guide. Spirit guided lucid dreaming has many possibilities and this is truly one of them. There is however a level of trust which is needed when approaching this method. You and your guide overtime will naturally create a loving bond. The more you call on him or her, the more they will answer to you and expand your awareness. Yes, of course at the beginning, you may feel such things like, "How can I trust him?," "Is this real?" or "Am I going crazy?" These thought processes are all completely normal reactions that can occur during the early stages. Do not worry. I felt this too. However, I believe now, from all of the wild adventures my guide and I have shared together, including all of the "Mirrored Awakenings" I have experienced, he is more than real. I trust him dearly, and our hearts are forever connected.

When you finally meet your guide within the dream world, and feel it's time for the next stage, simply ask your guide to help stabilise and transform your environment. Eventually the lucid dream will come to a close. You will have to be aware of this short window as it passes pretty rapidly. The lucid dream will start to decay around you and lose its energy. The colours will darken and the projections will began to take on a new look, usually similar to running paint on a canvas. Your dream vision will begin to blur and your orientation will be put to the test. This brief period is a great time to speak to your guide and ask him to prolong the dream and transcend your experience.

I've had many extended lucid dreams using this method. When I requested this, my spirit guide carefully placed his hands over my dream-head and I felt a big surge of energy and movement rushing through me. We'd plummet into the grounds of the existing dream into a wormhole and were projected deeply into the next realm.

The visual and feel of this particular anomaly could be associated to the movie Star Gate. When the marines enter the gate by pushing their faces into a pool of water-like substance, then instantly being pulled across space and time! This feeling took a few tries for me to adjust to, and in some respects you don't really get used to something of this magnitude. But then there is no fear; you hold tight to your guide and trust that when you submerge into the next realm everything will be divinely laid out for you.

Today, I still use this process with my guide. I really like the idea of not entirely knowing where I'll end up once we go through the wormhole. Similar to a DEILD, Dream Exit Induced Lucid Dream, (except, this way we don't wake up briefly before we return back to the dream world) I feel this is a more of an advanced way in translocation to another realm, with, of course, the help from a loving spirit guide.

That's part of the adventure though. To not fully know where your dream-self will end up next is always a wonderful mystery! This may be slightly daunting at first, especially while getting to know and trust your guide. There is an element of surrender that is needed on your behalf so trust your guide, for he has a great plan for you. It's actually quite a nice feeling! You both will emerge together into a new dream environment.

The new dreamscape seems to be similar to the astral realms. The textures, colours and structure seem more detailed, possibly because you have transcended into a higher vibration. You may feel slight tingles on your physical body, especially the head and spine area. I have discovered that the deeper I go and transcend my experience, the harder it is for me to remember in great detail what actually happened in the last realm. There seems to be slight risk of dream memory loss between transcending into the different realms.

Slight memory loss of the experience is not that bad, if you wish to just exercise your lucid dreaming muscle. You will however, remember in great detail the last realm you visited, but not so much the previous ones. Just to reiterate, I am not referring to your actual physical memory! Just the memory loss of the dream experiences themselves.

You will be more of an advanced dreamer the more you transition and recycle your lucidity. However, if you are on a mission to seek out new wisdom that you can bring back to the earthly realm, learn to transition with your guide responsibly. Expect your guide to have foreseen the future of where you will transition next. The guide will never put you in a position of threat or danger. Which raises the interesting question, is it then safe to assume that our spirit guides provide and orchestrate the direction within the actual wormhole?

Adapting to SGLD

Chapter Three

SGLD is a weird and wonderful type of lucidity that we can all apply. I believe today it's quite an uncommon occurrence relative to dream work. If you research the Internet, you will discover limited information out there about fusing these two wonders. Of course, there is countless litterateur that include spirit guides and conscious dreaming, but very little on Spirit Guided Lucid Dreaming. However, I do believe that more and more people are turning to their dreams for extra guidance and finding a spirit guide to further this even more will be the norm!

Firstly, when we are working with spirit energies within dreams, we need to understand their primordial nature. I was naturally an avid dreamer during my early stages and I was always keen to look deeper into unlocking the secrets of the mind; to go further into the depths of the subconscious mind and push the limits to the best of my ability. No matter how far I went, I always strove to remember that a subtle loving force was forever protecting and guiding me. Even if you don't feel like this now, do not worry. For they are watching you right now, waiting patiently and sending you guidance and love.

The spirit families are metaphysical beings and exist in alternate dimensions where linear time does not exist. The spirit watching over you could possibly be a dead relative who took an oath in watching over you during their crossover period. Or they could be a being from another solar system entirely, selected specifically for guiding your soul throughout your life on Earth. They could be a manifestation of your higher self to closely watch over you during the earthly years that you're alive. Every case is unique and yet all originating from the same source.

They can drift in and out of our reality as they please, back and forth into our consciousness and our dream world. They are guiding, advising and metaphysically orchestrating simulations and situations, in most cases on a subconscious level. All to help us grow more spiritually.

This does not mean we are simply puppets of a divine force, acting out pre-written life scripts. Far from it! Instead we are completely in charge of every passing thought and action. We always have a choice. We are in charge of our own destiny.

I have discovered that spirit guides simply influence our decisions for the better, and always offer the option not to take the advice if we do not wish to. The final thought process is always our decision depending on how much we wish to let them into our lives. They will never break the law of free will.

Through my research I have come to understand that each individual of the spirit group consist of a highly intelligent organisational system. Usually, the groups consist of five members. Each one is designated to a particular area in the makeup of our unique personalities.

For example, one may be working closely on our masculine qualities, another guiding our more feminine characteristics, another guiding our major interests and desires etc. They will then appear in the appropriate order depending on the stage of the individual's psychological/spiritual development. If you are looking for personal growth, spiritual or not, you may even request for the next teachings and your guide will send them directly to you through dreaming. We do so by setting our intention with the question in mind before we sleep.

Power of Thought

From the power of thought we attract what we want, but not just any wishy-washy thought. The thought should include a high, energetic vibration so that it can be created. Put simply, if we desire something strongly with great belief and intent, it shall be ours for the taking. Everything in the universe is made up of energy. All things are vibrating at different rates. So when we add 'energy' of a high capacity by including passion, our thoughts then become alive and formulate right in front of our eyes.

If we are to contact our spirit family, we must first understand the important rule of intention and its great power. This is how we first shift our awareness, lucidly thus attracting our spirit family. We have to make the effort and dedicate our time accordingly for it to be a reality.

Imagine this for a brief moment;

You, (the satellite) send out your intention with the power of thought (the transmission) and you beam it into the cosmos. The power of attraction (the receiving satellite) picks up your transmission, then decodes what you desire and bounces it back to earth so it can become a living reality. It's that simple. Be careful what you desire though, it is a powerful tool when mastered. So use this wisdom with utmost respect and love.

Having many lucid dreams is fun, for me as it is for many, I'm sure! Flying like Superman high in the sky, visiting the Taj Mahal for afternoon tea, diving headfirst into a mountain-high chocolate cake, hanging out with your favourite celebrities and acting out your wildest erotic fantasies etc. All of this can be achieved in lucid dreaming, just as if we were experiencing and controlling these experiences in waking life. This sounds great! Who wouldn't want to lucid dream?

The conscious mind is no longer limited to be enclosed in this shell we call the human body. The mind is not subject to physical matter and therefore can transport itself to any location outside the very boundaries of space and time, all by the power of thought.

As you progress through lucid dreaming, you may feel you have reached a limit, then you may wonder if there is a deeper truth to all that exists.

We can all move to the next big stage in conscious dreaming when we experience SGLD. I describe this like a fast-track lane to higher wisdom and peace.

However, I understand and respect that gaining such vast quantities of wisdom and spiritual evolution really depends on the practitioner. Only when your spirit guide feels you are ready for the next stage, will you be offered the opportunity for growth.

Looking through the clear glass of our inner and outer self with incredible high definition is really what's at the forefront with practicing SGLD. There is no comparison.

You will have a metaphysical best friend who has the skeleton key to open up all of the doors in the universe. You can call upon them anytime, which is within itself a real blessing. You will never feel alone, no matter how bad things get.

I can safely say that my life truly began to be awakened when I finally sealed the bond with my spirit guide. The feeling of being alone in this big world has vanished.

There is infinite wisdom to be gained out there, both internally and externally. Guidance is always there, if we choose to receive it.

Unlocking the secrets of the human mind fascinates many across the planet. If we didn't wonder such things, how would the human mind ever expand to a higher consciousness? How would the boundaries ever be pushed to think outside of the box? How would technology, science and medicine ever evolve? How would it have been possible for man to land on the moon? How would we fly in the sky, using huge winged machines that weigh many tons?

All of this is achieved firstly, by a single thought.

"If we can think it, then we can surely create it..."

The first stage in SGLD

The first stage in adapting your practice to SGLD, is to switch your mind and thought process to a place where you really believe that your guide is already presently with you. How is this done? There are many ways to beam out this unique intention and all will be revealed as you advance into your SGLD practice. You can make that first step right now if you like? It's very easy.

First, sit quietly and empty your thoughts. Do not close your eyes. Look around your surroundings and take in all that you see. Just observe. Become aware of your breathing, and breathe deeply in and out through your nose. Don't force any breath. Just be calm and relax into the moment. Observe any sounds you may hear, maybe the sound of a bird singing in the nearby trees perhaps.

Now ask in a calm loving voice,

"Spirit Guide... Please be with me right now and sit close to me." Now wait for a brief moment and listen. Ask again this time, feeling the energy that's all around you. Notice any sensations and scan all your senses. Surrender any doubt and learn to feel. Listen even more closely now, so that you can even hear a pin drop. Ask one more time,

"Spirit Guide... Please be with me right now and sit close to me."

Observe and sense your awareness expanding throughout the entire universe, being aware and connected to the physically unseen.

Congratulations! If you're wondering "what for?" Well, you've just made a huge step into consciously contacting your spirit guide. Even if you had no noticeable sensations or feelings, do not worry. Just the fact that you shifted your awareness into the direction of making contact is what counts with this exercise. You can be certain that your guide is pleased with whatever result you just experienced.

You may practice this technique any time throughout the day to strengthen the bond. You can say it to yourself whilst sitting at your desk at work. Maybe say it out loud whilst driving your car. Wherever and whenever is fine. Just before you sleep is also another great time as this will stay with you when you dream.

They can read our thoughts telepathically, so there's no need for concern about shouting out things aloud in public places where other people may feel uncomfortable. You can do this exercise when you're alone or with family, however, I suggest saying this aloud. I believe it makes the intention much stronger on a vibratory level and provides greater energy between you and your spirit companion. Remember that the goal is to reach the cosmos by including energy into the intention, so really believe your words and feel it! By doing this exercise daily you will feel a stronger presence around you and contact with your guide will be inevitable.

Adopting the right SGLD attitude

Finding your spirit family need not be a strain or pressure for you. Do not work against the natural universal energies, become frustrated and feel you will never succeed. This is not the attitude you need. Instead, understand in your heart, that the fact you are considering this practice at this time, showing keen interest in connecting to your sprit guide, more than proves that you are now ready to seek out your sacred helper. Your guide has influenced and presented opportunities your whole life for you to reach this stage, so be proud of your efforts so far.

When I first met my spirit guide officially in a lucid dream, I knew instantly that it was him. The more you search and dedicate time, setting your mindset towards reaching your guide and raising your awareness, the more chance you will have in finding them. It is not a question of if; it is simply a matter of when. Being in a constant lucid state, that is, always being aware of every given thought and action, in every moment, every breath and every second deep within your being, will eventually break down the illusory wall that separates us from the other worlds.

Exercise for SGLD Mindset

You can start to adapt this newly found attitude by doing the following exercise;

Take a stroll to a nearby forest where you can be alone and not be distracted. As you walk along the forest floor, observe any physical changes in your breath or muscular sensations. Just observe throughout this exercise. With deep slow inhalations, smell the air through your nose. Can you detect any scents? Open your ears and listen to your surroundings, what do you hear? Look above and notice the tree's leaves. Can you hear them rustling? Continue to keep walking at a steady pace, not too fast and not too slow, always moving. Observe your thoughts; are you feeling relaxed and at peace, more so than before? You may feel a loving energy in the distance? Can you feel any sensations? Do you feel safe?

As you are walking, imagine that this is all a dream. Everything around you is created by your subconscious mind. You have created this, every leaf and every flower.

Say to yourself, "I'm lucid in my dream! This is all a dream!" Really believe this to be true. Feel it and be excited like you normally would. Look around again and observe. How do you feel? Look around you and pause for a moment to touch the ground. Feel the soil and fallen leaves through your fingers. Notice how real it all feels!

Being in a state of mind where you truly feel that you are present in the moment, will open you up more intuitively. This is how you become receptive to your spirit guide's energy pattern. You will find, as you practice this formational foundation in awareness on a regular basis, strange events may spontaneously occur. Maybe, certain repetitive numbers will present themselves to you whilst in the checkout. You may read people's thoughts before they speak, hear a high pitched tone in one ear, see flashes of light in the corner of your eye, or sense a presence when you enter a room. These are just some of the many signs you will get accustomed to when you become more receptive to the spirit energies.

Training your Awareness

One thing to ask ourselves when observing spirits and dream characters is how can we be sure they are, who they say they are?

Other dream experiences have shown that if we ask three times to any character, they will honestly tell the truth on the third time. I have tried this method and it worked well. From it I had a direct conversation with my subconscious mind. A very surreal moment for me!

However, strangely I did not feel the need to try this with my spirit guide. With time and dedication you will begin to develop an extra-sensory tracking device in SGLD, deep within your dreaming mind. The more you harness its great power the more physic your awareness becomes. Before you know it, you can distinguish between the subconscious projections and the spirits automatically.

Even if they have different disguises impersonating people you may know, or appear to be extremely convincing! You will feel their unique presence.

The subconscious projections that I've encountered through the years share a distinctive characteristic that needs to be mentioned. If you look at a projected character deep into the eyes, they appear to have a glazed stare, not vibrant and coherent like a real spirit and in human eyes. They almost look through you like an android. This may differ in other people's dream world though. This is a great tool in searching for your guide to begin with. Through trial and error, discerning who's who with the help of noticing the eyes, has helped me progress significantly throughout my search.

There seems to be an unknown force that surrounds us all, much bigger than we could have ever have imagined. I feel, if we really wish to discover our spirit family, they will come and find us in our dreams regardless. Maybe our guides are already present within all of them, including our non-lucid dreams. Observing, as we sleep walk around the depth of our minds, in hope that one day, we will bring forth the loving attention they deserve.

If you are seeking your spirit guides through dreaming, it will most certainly take a great deal of passion and dedication on your part. They will not suddenly appear in front of you if you don't wish for them to be seen in the first place. With a greater effort to pinpoint your spirit guide's energy and to use a sense of feeling guided from your natural intuition, you'll be carrying a beacon of light wherever you decide to dreamwalk. It will eventually become second nature to you. You have to trust your inner-self implicitly for this to work. For when you fully trust, the unseen energies begin to appear.

Clifftoft once told me that in order to open myself up more psychically, I would first need to understand that all of this is achieved by 'feeling.' To feel instead of perceiving fully with our logical self, is how we reactivate and operate the psychic self within us. It is the prime foundation for gaining extra-sensory cognitive skills within dream and wake.

It took me many months to truly understand what he meant by the use of feeling. My spirit guide then orchestrated a lucid dream one moonlit night which helped me understand this further;

I'm in a large mansion, standing with friends in a living room watching a big television screen on the wall. I am lucid. I can see a man on the screen reading the weather forecast. I feel a sensation that cannot be put into words. Curiosity about whom that man was creeps over me like a warm blanket. I take a leap of faith and say aloud his remaining dialogue! Why I feel compelled to, I do not know. "We are completely in sync!" I say aloud. I am astonished! Now I can see it is my guide impersonating a weather reader. As I come to realise, I say, "Hey, Clifftoft! I knew it was you!!" The weather man and I smile at what I just discovered. I am really pleased that I guessed it correctly! I feel I can see through any disguise my guide presents to me.

From this lucid dream, I seem to have developed a heightened sense of telepathy. I took a leap into the unknown, followed my intuition and learned to feel instead of think. Now my guide and I talk telepathically every day and as a result I can feel his powerful presence.

Him orchestrating this SGLD, to test my senses, made me more perceptive to his specific telepathic frequency. Today, I notice that my telepathic awareness has definitely increased since discovering SGLD. As we unlock the barrier in communicating to our guides telepathically, this will have a knock-on effect into our physical world and expand our psychic centers even further.

We can unlock the secrets of the mind and gain incredible cognitive skills within our dream world, then bring those skills back into waking reality. The secret powers within us seem to always be present. It is just locked behind a door that's hidden deep within our subconscious minds. It's waiting for us to find and turn that key, so we can unlock its spectacular prize. Our guides offer a master key to open these many doors.

SGLD Preparation

After adopting the correct mindset and understanding the power of intention, we can begin to move to the next stage and implement some basic preparations to setup our practice in being more successful.

Of course if you are already an avid dreamer, you'll understand the importance of a dream journal. It is a journal that can assist your practice and shed new light, masses of wisdom, insight into your spiritual self and help you maintain a connection to your dream studies. Using your dream journal devotedly will also strengthen your ability to lucid dream.

Reality checks throughout the day are essential when tearing down the wall between dream and wake. Questioning our waking reality many times throughout the day, as well as a short test to check the reality, will eventually creep into our subconscious minds. We will then be more coherent within the dream and be highly lucid. The test I really prefer is to check the palm of my hands. I try to push a finger into the center of my palm to see if it goes through or not. If it does, then you can be sure you are dreaming! Really ask yourself before you test it out, "Am I Dreaming?" You can always set yourself an hourly chime on a digital watch to remind you.

SGLD Diet

By including a fresh and high-vibrant diet into our lives, we can be sure to accumulate wondrous health benefits, as well as accelerating our own cognitive senses. The messages we receive from spirits can be easily heard when we are a clear channel. So our bodies need to be clean and healthy. The saying "we are what we eat" has a lot of meaning if you think about it! When we eat lighter and cleaner, i.e. fresh vegetables and fruits, we feel lighter and happier. We don't want to be eating heavy meals late at night, this will leave us feeling bloated and flat and down in our moods. Eat light, eat clean and be well is our aim.

Among many other factors, having a more alkaline diet is useful. Our blood is naturally 7.36 pH, which makes our bodily systems slightly alkaline. Today, the modern western diet consists of high sugars, heavy salts, pre-packaged ready meals, artificial additives, hormone injected meats and processed dairy. All of which are considered highly toxic to our bodies.

Reducing, or even better, cutting out these foods completely, will positively boost our health, bringing us closer to spirit. Most spirit mediums and psychics of the world are vegetarian; this explains why they all have made that lifestyle choice.

My spirit guide once told me, that I would need to be a clear channel in order to hear him clearly. Our guidance transmission is extremely sensitive to the foods we eat. The cleaner we eat, the clearer the transmission will be from our spirit guide. The vital organs will be operating at optimal level once there're cleared of toxins. Your mood will then be uplifted, you will gain a great sense of wellbeing, feel more creative, have tons more energy than before, heightened intelligence and be more sensitive psychically to the spirit energies.

For a healthy balance, our diets should consist of about 80 percent alkaline foods to 20 percent acidic foods. Having too much acidity will cause toxaemia in our bodies that then leads to diseases such as cancer, osteoporosis, heart disease, arthritis, urinary disease, diabetes and others. We don't have to be fully vegetarian or vegan, but as close to the 80 percent intake of alkaline foods, the better.

White bread, pastries, pasta, white rice, fast food, processed and packaged foods and animal products etc will eventually convert into more acidity in the body.

We overcome this by eating more simply, using fresh ingredients as natural as possible. Green leafy vegetables that are lightly steamed, wholesome grains, nuts and seeds, fresh fruits and water are all a great way to clean out all of the accumulated toxic sludge that has been building up over the years. Your digestion and vital organs will love you even more after you've started to eat this way. Your dreams will most certainly become more vivid, you will need less sleep and your energy levels and mind will be beautifully in balance. Fasting for a few days on either mineral water or fresh fruit is another wonderful way to clear out the system. Three-day fasts are not so demanding, and highly effective when clearing out the toxic backlog.

We must look after our bodies like they always look after us. The human body is constantly ridding itself of toxins and pathogens. It always strives toward self-healing to bring it into equilibrium once again. By eating and drinking in a clean and simple fashion, your body will also have a chance to catch up and rid itself from any physical and emotional discord.

Supplements that assist Dreaming

Throughout history, records indicate that natural herbs and plants have been used to facilitate altered states of consciousness. For instance, to make your dreams significantly more vivid and memorable, you may place Mugwort under your pillow. You could use a few drops of lavender essential oil to insure a deep, non-interrupted sleep where vivid dreams begin to surface.

Below is a list of different plants and flowers that can help you with your dream studies. You may even make a dream pillow from the herbs listed below and place it near to where you sleep;

Lavender, star tulip, mugwort, white chestnut, dill, apple coleus, jimson weed, gum plant, litchi, orange, owl's clover, St Johns wort, forget-me-not, rabbitbrush, chestnut bud, Queen Anne's lace, pashion flower and calea zacatechichi.

My Favourite Dream Herb

This has to be my personal favourite dream herb of all time! Some of my best SGLD experiences were from taking this herb. Galantamine has become known as the lucid dreaming pill. It is an alkaloid synthesised from the red spider lily plant. It greatly increases our chances by assisting us in staying on the tipping point between wake and sleep, whilst promoting an important neurotransmitter, acetylcholine. Galatamine is widely associated with a Wake Initiated Lucid Dream. The results are significantly increased if we combine the herb with choline bitartrate. I have a premade blend of 4mg Galantamine, 200mg of choline, per capsule. I take two capsules in a "wake back to bed method" and in the early hours of the morning around 4 am.

This can be a fantastic way to induce lucid dreaming and can remove any mental blocks that may be hindering your progress. However, it is also important to remember that we mustn't solely rely on taking the supplement to reach a state of lucidity. Sure, ingesting them will improve our skill in becoming lucid, but like with all dreaming aids, we should intuitively go with our gut instinct, understanding and respecting the traditional foundational methods too.

SGLD Crystals and Gemstones

Throughout some of my dreams with my guide, I was shown images of certain stones and crystals that will help me keep the channel to my spirit open and receptive. I discovered that a certain crystal and gemstone could bring me an abundance of cognitive help and healing. Two in particular are labradorite (gemstone) and selenite (crystal). They are both now a part of my SGLD study and I highly recommend you carry them in some form.

The stones are available to buy as a pendant or as a pebble so it can be placed into your pocket. Whether or not you believe in the power of crystals and stones is not important. By holding them with you for just one day, you will be sure to notice their great unique energies. I believe it is always good to keep an open mind about the natural forces, and experience them on a personal level so you can identify and make your own judgment.

Labradorite relieves anxiety, hopelessness and depression, replacing them with enthusiasm, self-confidence and inspiration. It is said to dispel negativity and to bring clear understanding by enhancing clarity of thought and improving one's ability to cooperate with others in harmony. Labradorite is also said to give perseverance, strength and enhanced intuition when one is experiencing times of conflict and change. Labradorite is said to be helpful in treating eye and brain disorders, and to help regulate metabolism and the digestive process.

If you place a small pebble of labradorite under your pillow at night, you may experience astral travel and lucid dreams. Regular dreams also become extremely vivid. The gemstone seems to bring added awareness and energy to your dream self. I use my labradorite gemstone frequently. Once a week I will charge the gemstone in the sun while submerged in mineral water for a day or so. This will guarantee the gemstone will be full of the sun's energy.

Figure 3 Labradorite

Selenite (fig.3) is said to be a powerful crystal for psychic communication. It will aid in interaction with the wise ancestors, angels and spirit guides as well as loved ones. It is said to do this telepathically and through divination. It is therefore a stone that can be used by mediums, clairvoyants and SGLD practitioners. Translucent selenite has a very fine vibration and shall bring clarity of mind, opening the crown and higher chakras while accessing angelic consciousness and higher guidance. Pure selenite is a link to the light body, helping to anchor it in the earth vibration. I use a small piece of selenite attached to a necklace to keep me close to my guide. It is important never to immerse the crystal into water. It really doesn't like water! Just charging it in the sun on its own will give it power again.

Figure 4 Selenite

Physical Practices

Regular exercise of the body in some form or another will facilitate SGLD. There are of course many to choose from out there. Like all exercise, a little bit everyday will add years onto your life.

Sometimes, the most effective exercises are the simplest. Basic stretching before you sleep, massaging certain acupuncture points on the body and the use of hand formations called mudras can really help your lucidity.

Learning a form like Qigong or Tai Chi (a Chinese physical practice of energy) can balance any emotional, spiritual and physical ailments you may have. The balance of the internal yin-yang energies within our bodies is essential for SGLD. Practicing basic movements daily will help you towards connecting with Spirit. I have been studying and practicing a form of Qigong. I can affirm of its countless benefits, physically, emotionally and spiritually.

Slow relaxing movements and breathing techniques are among of the key ingredients to Qigong. My guide showed me this ancient art through a series of many dreams, making me understand its true potential. I understand that my dream's message was exclusively for me and may not be for everyone. But if you feel you wish to discover a deeper aspect of yourself, connect with Mother Nature more and feel the cosmos running through your body, then I recommend this physical practice. My dreams have taken on a whole new level now I practice Qigong. I seem to be able to hear my guide even better now, expanding simultaneously my awareness and spirituality.

Balancing Exercise

One way of creating such a pose is to first stand on a flat surface with arms facing down and your feet separated slightly. Then bend your left leg back and grab your ankle with your right hand. Make sure to bend enough so the back of the heel of the foot is against your backside. Raise your remaining arm high into the sky, fingers point up. Retain this strong stance for a minute or so. Now try it the opposite way. After you have done this a few times, you will feel a great sense of inner and outer balance. Continue swapping sides for as long you need.

Your brain's hemispheres will become more balanced than before and as a result will heighten your lucid dreaming. Records now show that athletes who perform gymnastics are naturally, frequent lucid dreamers! This is probably one of the reasons why Qigong is also highly effective for lucid dreaming, because there are many balancing poses, bringing synchronicity to both sides of the brain.

Dream Journal- Your Personal Gateway to Wisdom

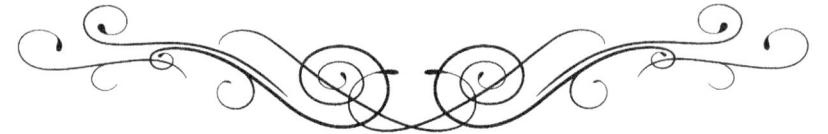

Chapter Four

Your dream experiences, no matter how big or small, should all be placed into a dream journal. At first keeping a journal can be a bit of a chore and you may sometimes forget to write down experiences. However in time you will realise how much of a necessity keeping a dream journal really is, and writing in entries every morning becomes a pleasure!

My journal is my most important tool. It unlocks all the wondrous secrets of the psyche and dream patterns suddenly emerge. In time you will more clearly detect the symbolic nature of your subconscious mind and what it is communicating to you.

You will be able to identify your "dream signs." Is there anything in particular that is reoccurring and unusual? Maybe a certain childhood memory or familiar place?

The symbolic nature of our dreams can tell us a huge amount. As soon as we put focus on recording our dreams daily, we begin to grow and the significance of our dreams expand. Your awareness becomes crisper and more coherent.

Many people have reported increased dream memory by recording their dreams as soon as they wake. You can wait till morning; only you then risk not including all of the dream's fine details. Make sure when you awaken that you don't move from your bed position. Changing your posture in bed immediately after waking will greatly decrease your memory of the dream! Whilst not moving, say to yourself that you will remember everything from this dream. Now cast your mind back and recall all the events of your experience. When you're ready to move, pickup your journal and proceed to write it down.

Ideal Dream Journal Features:

Date: Write the date of the morning you had the dream (the same date as when you awaken)

Time Within Dream: Write down the time it 'felt' like in the dream. Obviously time has no meaning in the dream world but it somehow prepares your lucid mind to stay lucid longer.

Trigger: Try to remember the crucial point that triggered you into lucidity. Maybe just before you felt a certain emotion perhaps?

Location/Landscape: Describe what dreamscape surrounds you and what it reminds you of, maybe a type of particular building or from a past memory, etc.

Spirits/Projections: State here whom you interacted with. Write down any familiar faces you've seen before. Is it a spirit or a subconscious projection?

Dream Symbols/Objects: Any particular object or weird thing stand out? Any certain colours, emotions, bodily occurrences, interesting building structures, sound etc. What symbology did you see?

Emotions: Examine how you felt during the dream. What emotion(s) did you experience? What do you feel now you are awake?

Experience: Describe from the beginning your lucid or non-lucid dream experience. Use simple and concise wording when writing in your entries.

Always write in the present tense instead of using past tense.

For example, you would write, "I'm walking down this street and I see a man"

As opposed to, "I walked down this street and saw a man." By writing in the present tense, you will be able to remember even more details of your dream as you are recording them.

Conclusion: This section can be completed at a later date or the day after if you wish whilst the memory is still fresh in your mind. This is where you can dissect and analyse what your dream was trying to tell you, from the people you met to the perceptions and objects you encountered. What did your dream symbols tell you?

Occurrences & Objects

I find underlining the main key words within the experience really helps me when trying to decipher the dream's encryption. This gives me easy access when quickly referencing my dream meanings.

For example you may have written,

"I'm running up a steep hill and I see a red flag which makes me feel happy"

Here is what stood out:

"I'm **running up** a **steep hill** and I see a **red flag** which makes me **feel happy**"

This is where you can start to see emerging patterns and symbolic meanings that can be understood. There are many books on dream interpretations and thousands of websites that offer dream dictionaries. At the end of the day, only you can interpret the true meaning of what you feel from the experience intuitively. Trust in your higher self to get the answers you seek.

Lastly I place a little box in the top, right hand corner of the page where I write what type of dream it was. This really helps you gauge your progress whilst quickly flicking through your journal. It also pushes you mentally to achieve more if you're not satisfied with the results.

I use this method of abbreviation when labeling the dream's type:

(L) 'Lucid'- Full lucidity is when one is fully conscious that one is dreaming within a dream and recognises the physical body simultaneously coexisting back on earth.

(SL) Semi Lucid- is when you're aware that you're dreaming but believe that this is the only version of you existing within the present dream. You have no sense of a physical life on Earth and are at risk of re-entering a non-lucid state.

(NL) 'Non-Lucid'- is commonly known today as a regular dream. You play out an entire script and are completely unaware that you are dreaming.

(VD) 'Vivid Dream'- Very much like a non-lucid dream in a sense of being unaware one is dreaming but this time everything is completely vivid and real. Your interactions are extremely realistic and can be deemed as "Earth-like," your senses are completely heightened and the tactile sensations are extremely real.

(OBE) 'Out Of Body Experience'- is when the spirit (energy body/soul) leaves its physical body and can project outwards to anywhere within the astral planes.

Objective Setting

I thought I'd include objective setting within this chapter because it can be an added to our dream journals. When we consciously connect to our spirit guide, we gain a great sense in knowing that the unachievable is now attainable, any goal we set ourselves is more than possible!

Writing a list of goals and desires is a great way to inwardly confirming to yourself, that this is within reach. When we write any form of text down, when the pen hits the paper, our subconscious part of ourselves recognises and records this.

Our journals can be so much more, if we use them also for objective setting. I have found the most success with placing goals/objectives into my journal. I use a page towards the back and simply write down twenty to thirty goals that I wish to achieve. There I write them down and my guide watches as I do this. For example, some of the ones I listed last year include, "Unlock my psychic abilities even more," "Meet my deceased grandparents," "Be more in tune with Mother Earth" and so on. All of those objectives have now been answered and those lucid experiences blew me away. The objective setting seemed to keep my focus throughout. Especially when I had a mission to complete.

From there, you will find that they will start to receive spontaneous answers, in dream or physical reality. You will be faced with odd situations, meet certain people at the right time to help you on your quest, prophetic dreams will appear and extra-ordinary capabilities will grow within you. These are just some of the many attributes objective setting has to offer.

Another way to make a specific intention to manifest, especially for lucid dreaming, is to write down the objective/question many times repeatedly on the page. I write about twenty-five lines of the same objective. Although it can be repetitive, you will find if done before you sleep, this will incubate its vibration into your next coming dream. This is a great way in directly receiving the answers we are searching for. You can also practice this method for SGLD. You could write twenty-five to thirty times an intention such as, "I now find my spirit guide in my lucid dreams." Continue to write the specific goal consistently throughout many days, to get this direct message to your subconscious mind. It's about making something repetitive, and easy to understand, so don't write long-winded dissertations in your method of writing. You will need a big dream journal if you do! You will be fine as long as it's simple, concise and clear.

SGLD Techniques & Traditional Methods

Chapter Five

Over the years I have tried all kinds of weird and wonderful ways to induce the lucid state. As there are so many techniques out there, usually the practitioner in the early stages will discover a special favourite for achieving lucidity. The fact is that there is no definite "one way solution" that will please all. That's not to say however that you can't increase your chances in lucidity by applying the right preparation and correct mindset first to maximise your chances. With time and dedication you're guaranteed success. Furthermore, you will discover which techniques really resonate with you and not put time and energy into the ones that don't. By having perseverance and focused goals, you will achieve great lucidity; so don't give up at the first hurdle!

Within this chapter, I have included the traditional mainstream techniques for lucid dreaming first. This is so that any dreamer, at a novice level, can start to build a healthy foundational practice into lucid dreaming. For the advanced dreamers out there, this is a good way to revise your way through some of the old methods to refine your practice. I believe sometimes, being experienced lucid dreamers, we tend to forget over time what we originally learned. It's good to remind ourselves to strengthen our skill.

It is important however, if you are a beginner, to make sure you at least have multiple successful lucid dreams by using the traditional techniques first. Either traditional method is fine. The SGLD methods will need to follow the basic techniques once mastered, otherwise you will not fully grasp the true concept in meeting your guide through dreaming. As mentioned previously, we need to energetically open ourselves up so that we're in harmony with the universal energy. We will then be a clear channel and be that incredibly bright beacon of light so that our guides can locate us. More accurately, we will be able to locate them.

We accelerate towards this by first becoming accustomed to the original teachings of lucidity; we can then proceed in a healthy and respectful manner.

The SGLD techniques that are listed below were given to me intuitively from my guide, through the means of dream, meditation and dream-incubation. Some may call this a form of channeling. Call it what you will, I prefer to understand it as a form of SGLD. You will find that as you progress and speak to your guide regularly, the transmission between you and spirit will become very strong. You will receive new insights and cognitive formed thought patterns that are from the highest source within you. That highest source, I believe, is your spirit guide.

There have been many times I've experienced the familiar sensation of my guide. I walk into a room, I relax my mind, I happen to skim a small concern over in my mind briefly. I then receive an instantaneous phrase or sometimes an image that demonstrates a solution! I check to confirm that the source of this instant solution was my guide. I check this by using, what I call, a "Mirrored Awakening." Yes! I am right. I can confirm now when he is around influencing my thought patterns and offering his guidance. You too can develop a checking system for you and your guide. I will explain this in greater detail in chapter eight.

Strangely enough, the more you notice the signs, the stronger the bond becomes between you and spirit. I now sense him around and we are both completely locked into each other telepathically, physically, emotionally and spiritually. This won't take long at all if you are willing to not judge yourself and the information presented here. Only you can determine what you wish to manifest into your life. This is why I repeatedly speak of letting go and allowing. Trusting in the unseen to become seen, is the message I give to you with all my heart. Living in this state of being is the ultimate key in accessing the spirit guide within you. We must be neutral in the mind, come from a place of love and have clear thinking if we are to hear them.

Essential Preparations

Before we go steaming ahead with techniques and discovering wonderful ways to trigger lucidity, there are some initial guidelines we should take into consideration:

Create a safe haven where you will be practicing/sleeping. For many people this is your bedroom area. You may wish to scent your pillows with lavender oil to relax you even more. Lavender will also help open the channel between you and your spirit guides.

Write down any concerns or doubts on a piece of paper and transform them by positively affirming them. For example, "I will remember my dreams." This will give your mind and subconscious a chance to release any fears and doubts you may have accumulated over time. This is useful and relaxing becomes easy from here on.

Become accustomed to generally relaxing and resting in the daytime. Sounds easy right? But can be a little tricky if you're not used to it. The nap in the day, should not be overlooked. Try taking afternoon Siestas around 1-3 pm for really no longer than forty-five minutes at a time. This will quiet your mind significantly and is scientifically proved to return your brain back to optimal levels again. As a result, intelligence, focus and mood are greatly enhanced.

If you wish to catapult your lucid dreaming skills to the next level, you need to meditate. You do not have to learn meditation; you just simply 'be' meditation. You can do this in the morning, in the afternoon and at night. Whenever, wherever is fine. Whatever feels right, is right. There is no pressure at all with meditation. Once you feel the benefits and notice that your dreams are becoming even more real, you will dedicate time and practice into meditation diligently, (if you have not done so already that is.)

Here is a way to focus the mind: Sit in a quiet, darkened room, no disturbances or sounds, close your eyes, cross your legs if you prefer and clasp your hands. Breathe deeply in through your nose and out through your mouth to clear away any unwanted thoughts and concerns. Try to empty your mind. Imagine a blue sky filling your vision. Each fluffy white cloud represents a thought. Every time you exhale, a cloud (or thought) will drift away. Eventually, all the clouds will have vanished and you will be left with a beautiful clear blue sky and have pure clarity of the mind.

Remain in a peaceful state during the day. Avoid any confrontations or chaotic traffic jams that will make you upset and angry. The more serene and calm your mind is during the day, the easier it will be for you to lucid dream at night.

Throughout your day, on the hour, affirm repeatedly to yourself, "I now Lucid Dream." (Being in the present tense is much more effective for your subconscious to recognise.)

See all life as a dream. Look around and really believe that you are in a lucid dream. Observe your surroundings with great belief and curiosity. If you see a person, question (to yourself) if they're created from your subconscious mind, or if they might be a spirit from another world checking in on you. Have this unique viewpoint always in the back of your head during the events of your day. Practice this mindset until it becomes a natural part of your lifestyle.

Set an alarm clock to wake you at 4 am if you don't do so naturally. Not all methods require this time in waking, but it is the most preferred, as it's generally the perfect period for lucid dreaming. It will increase your chances.

Make sure there are no sudden noises that can disturb you whilst you practice and sleep. Try wearing earplugs if you live in a loud area.

Sleep masks are wonderful for lucid dreaming. You tend to have a deeper sleep when your sight is completely darkened because more melatonin is formed. Having some light is generally okay, as long as it doesn't hinder you sleeping at night.

Go to bed generally at a reasonably hour. (Aim for waking at 4:00 am naturally to practice WBTB method.)

Don't consume any stimulants such as caffeine, alcohol and drugs for obvious reasons. Green tea is a great coffee substitute and can also promote lucid dreaming too!

Watching TV/movies, playing video games etc. a few hours before bed will diminish your dreaming capability significantly, so try to stick to a cut-off point. As an alternative, why not try reading a book about lucid dreaming instead; it's a great way to relax and will strengthen your intention to be lucid in your dreams.

Make sure your sleeping quarters are at a comfortable temperature.

Wear loose or no clothes for bed. The more comfortable you are, the better.

Wearing socks can improve your sleep. If your feet are too hot then do without.

Make sure you have an open page ready from your dream journal, along with a pen (use the same one every time), a small flash light (or similar light source). The less you have to do in the middle of the night the better!

Burn wild sage around your bedroom, and clear away any old energetic debris that don't serve you. Not only will burning wild sage before bed bring you more vivid dreams; it is purifying for the energies and atmosphere. The transmission between you and spirit will now be open.

Traditional Techniques

Many studies over the years have shown which techniques have the biggest success rates. For instance, the Wake Back To Bed method (WBTB) is very efficient among many lucid dreamers. I still find myself revisiting the traditional techniques as a foundational basis in my practice even today. I believe it's essential in maintaining the focus of the mind. If we get sloppy with our practice, thus forgetting to use mantras or never really interrupt our sleep cycle in any way, we will never have a real shot in being regularly lucid. So even for the advanced dreamers out there, these methods are just as important compared to the modern-day ones.

The Mild Technique

The MILD technique, or Mnemonic Induction of Lucid Dreams, employs prospective memory, remembering to do something (notice you're dreaming) in the future. Dr. Stephen LaBerge developed this technique for his doctoral dissertation and used it to achieve lucid dreaming at will. The proper time to practice MILD is after awakening from a dream, before returning to sleep.

For me, this technique served as a great foundation for the start of my dream studies because it trains the subconscious mind to focus on an intention. I still use this at times depending on what my body wants. I believe it is always good to vary your methods so that you keep your subconscious mind entertained. The subconscious mind adores thoughts and intentions that are repetitive, simple and clear in nature. It recognises and orchestrates its communication to you in the language of symbology. When you constantly use the same technique over and over, it will adapt and may sometimes (not always) work against you. You somehow build a tolerance for the method. So the secret is to use a few of your favourite different methods and alternate them throughout the week. This may prove to be more successful for you.

Method

Setup dream recall. Set your mind through intention to awaken from dreams and recall them. When you awaken from a dream, recall it as completely as you can.

Focus your intent. While returning to sleep, concentrate single-mindedly on your intention to recognise that you're dreaming. Tell yourself: "Next time I'm dreaming, I will remember I'm dreaming," repeatedly, like a mantra. Put real meaning into the words and focus on this idea alone. If you find yourself thinking about anything else, let it go and bring your mind back to your intention.

See yourself becoming lucid. As you continue to focus on your intention to remember when you're dreaming, imagine that you are back in the dream from which you just awakened (or another one you have had recently if you didn't remember your most recent). Imagine that this time you recognise that you are dreaming. Look for a dream sign, something in the dream that demonstrates plainly that it is a dream. When you see it, say to yourself: "I'm dreaming!" and continue your fantasy. Imagine yourself carrying out your plans for your next lucid dream. For example, if you want to fly in your lucid dream, imagine yourself flying after you come to the point in your fantasy when you become lucid.

Repeat until your intention is set. Repeat steps 2 and 3 until either you fall asleep or are sure that your intention is set. If, while falling asleep, you find yourself thinking of anything else, repeat the procedure so that the last thing in your mind before falling asleep is your intention to recognise the next time you are dreaming.

Wake Back to Bed (WBTB)

Many lucid dreamers know that in the early hours of the morning, around 4am - 6am, is when your brain occupies the highest levels of serotonin and melatonin. This makes your chances in becoming lucid extremely high! Why not have all the best odds in your favour?

This particular time in the morning is when our dreams are most vivid and memorable. Studies show that roughly around this time, we experience Rapid Eye Movement or the REM period, one of the many phases we experience during the course of a night's sleep.

They call this next method the Wake Back To Bed Method (WBTB). Here it is with a few minor improvements of my own!

Method

Go to bed as normal (preferably 10 pm). Set your intention whilst sitting up in bed with closed eyes and clear your mind. Repeat the following to yourself for ten to fifteen minutes, "When I dream, I will know I'm dreaming."

Allow yourself to sleep for six hours. Set your alarm clock (if need be) to wake you up at 4 am.

After five to six hours, fully get out of bed and half wake up (the fewer lights that are turned on the better—I use a torch so I don't fully wake up!). Get up and use the toilet if need be, drink a glass of water and occupy your brain with reading about lucid dreaming. I prefer to go back to bed after a quick toilet break and prop myself up with pillows and meditate on the intention, "When I dream, I will know I'm dreaming." Do this for twenty to forty-five minutes.

Fall back down into bed and move the pillows to their original place and relax. If your mind is too alert, practice breathing slowly deep into the lower belly and through your nose. With every exhalation, relax a little more. Feel your entire body drifting back to a state of sleep with a memory of the intention.

Please Note:

You may use visualisations as well if you prefer. It can be distracting, however, if you have never tried this, cast your mind's memory back into the dreamscape and plan your next lucid dream as you fall asleep. The idea is to fall asleep again so try not to get too excited about what will happen next, this will work against you. Just try to relax and fall asleep again with the general intention or visualisation in mind.

The DILD Technique

Spontaneous lucid dreams can occur from time to time when we dream normally. Most people, whether they can remember it or not, have experienced a type of lucidity before. The DILD or Dream Induced Lucid Dream method trains the mind to notice within the dream state, that you are actually dreaming and thus can become lucid. This method is fairly common among dreamers and is fairly easy to achieve.

Method

Work on building your dream recall first by recording many daily entries into your dream journal. (This applies with all methods)

Meditate throughout the day and before you sleep to still the mind.

Perform daily routine reality checks to question whether or not you are in a dream.

As you fall asleep, repeat a chosen phrase that programs your subconscious to lucid dream. You may consider, "I will know when I'm dreaming," "I now have a lucid dream" or "I now do a reality check," etc.

The DEILD Technique

The DEILD or Dream Exit Induced Lucid Dream method happens to be one of my personal favourites. Once you master this method you can lucid dream all night. This method aids you in extending your experience to another lucid dream once the old dream has ended. Every dream, no matter how big or small has a certain life expectancy. As a dream ends, when we are lucid, we will notice a sudden degradation within our visual. Your dream self may become weak and darkness begins to surround you. At this stage we have an opportunity to extend our awareness to the next dream if we so wish to. Here's how it's done.

Method

When you're in bed about to sleep, set your intention to not move at all when awakening after a dream in the night. Firmly repeat to yourself, "I don't move after waking from my dream." Do this until it is firmly set in your mind, now drift off to sleep.

Your subconscious will now automatically awaken you in the night after a dream. Remember to not move at this stage. Remain keeping your eyes shut and retain your sleeping posture. If you accidently twitch a muscle or move your head, all progress will be reset and you will have to start all over again from the beginning.

From not moving, say immediately to yourself (repeatedly) your mantra, such as, "I'm now in a lucid dream" over and over again.

You will find that within an approximate time of ten seconds or so, you will be transported back into the next dream, fully lucid.

The WILD Technique

The WILD technique, or Wake Initiated Lucid Dream has been labeled the holy grail of all methods. In my past experience, I can vouch for such claims. It really is an intrinsic yet approachable technique. Once mastered, the remaining methods almost seem a walk in the park. The WILD technique is, in simple terms, not experiencing a lapse in one's consciousness from waking to sleep. The dreamer will then cross over, possibly having an out-of-body experience or will fall directly into the dream fully aware, fully lucid. This technique is one of the most popular methods today.

Method

If you have used the preparation guidelines stated previously, you have now greatly increased your chances in being successful. Securing a relaxing dream environment is essential for this practice and mustn't be carelessly overlooked. Accompanied daily meditational practice, for sharpening the mind's intent to be lucid, is necessary for all methods.

Similar to the WBTB method, you need to awaken around five to six hours after going to sleep. This applies only if you are to go to bed at night. If you are taking an afternoon nap, this is not really necessary. For example, if you go to bed at 10 pm, plan to awaken between the hours of 3 am – 4 am. You may set an alarm if you're not accustomed to waking naturally at this time. If you don't want to awaken your partner, you may use a vibrating alarm wristwatch which is available in most stores. If you don't like it on your wrist, you can always strap it to your ankle instead.

Upon awakening at night, make sure to rise fully out of bed and use the toilet if need be. An empty bladder is a happy bladder and won't distract you from your lucid adventures! Now pop back into bed whilst setting your intention to be lucid.

Lying down in any position is fine, as long as you're relaxed and try not to move. Remove any itching and annoyances etc. and breathe deeply. You can stretch your main muscle groups and release them individually whilst exhaling slow breaths. Relax deeply as you breathe. Let go of any passing thoughts. If you find your self thinking about anything in particular, don't analyse it in great detail, just observe in a nonjudgmental fashion. We want to avoid any inner-conflict with ourselves regardless of method. Being in a state of curiosity and lenient attitude, being innocent like a child, is ideal. Be pure of thought and full of love in your heart.

You may now see a few things within the black screen of your vision. This is to be expected. Do not put great attention on these images, as they will distract you from your progress. Instead, observe them as though you were glancing at a big cinema screen. Register them in your mind and then swiftly release them. This may take a few tries to get used to, but once you're familiar, it will become an interesting part of the journey.

As these physical and visual indicators increase, be sure to repeat your chosen mantra. You may use something that affirms the dream state like, "I am dreaming." If you like, you may include a count from one. This will keep your concentration on the task so you don't risk falling asleep and missing your golden window. Please remember, the trick is to remain focused through to the very point of exiting and to always remain completely relaxed, not forcing our way out.

You will start to notice that because you're repeating your chosen phrase and continuing to relax, the sensations and visuals will increase. What many dreamers report from this point on can vary. Some call it the astral tunnel. Others simply hear high-frequency sounds or feel bodily sensations. Everyone experiences something different. Full sleep paralysis by this stage, is fully activated. Don't be alarmed, this is a good thing. Strange physical sensations may increase as you feel you are nearly reaching this climax. Keep focusing on repeating your numbered phrase and don't be distracted, no matter what cause!

As this increases, indications will show you that you've reached the beginning of the next stage. Intuitively you will know when this is. You may use an exit technique to release your astral body, or simply intend to rise out. There are many exits available. Essentially, you want to perform a non-physical movement of lifting or rising.

I have discovered that it's non-physical movement that stimulates and activates the exiting process. For example, if we imagine a rope above our heads, we may start to climb it and place our hands firmly around it one by one and begin to lift ourselves out gradually.

I believe whatever instinctual method you use, don't hesitate to call upon your guides at this point for extra help. Even though you may not have fully met your spirit guide, they are sitting right next to you, waiting for you to ask and acknowledge them. They will gladly lift you out of your physical body with a kind tug if need be! When your dream self awakens, you'll have been transported into the other realms, fully lucid. Don't forget to call upon your spirit guide when you get there.

Intermittent Timer Technique

The timer method can have astonishing results, even in the first attempt to reach lucidity. It mainly activates sleep paralysis within the body and keeps your mind awake and your body asleep. You will enter into the in-between state of consciousness. This then leads to O.B.Es and lucid dreams. Out of all the methods, this is probably the easiest of them all, because it requires minimal effort from the dreamer.

The flash timer is used during the early hours of the morning, combined with the WBTB method. The timer is comprised of a series of intermittent beeps during certain intervals in multiples of 2, 3, 4, 5, or 6-minute ramps. Nicolas Newport from lucidology describes the timer method in great detail on his website. He has kindly condensed years of research into many presentations (Lucidology 101) and demonstrates how effective the timer can be for lucid dreaming.

The most commonly used setting for this timer, which is the setting by default when you open the flash file, is Ramp 4 (multiples of four minutes). Similar to the DEILD, the idea is not to move a muscle whilst the sleep paralysis is brought on, or this will delay your progress. When you hear the beep, don't move but try to fall asleep—it's that easy! You'll discover multiple high-level lucid dreams and O.B.Es. This is recommended for the dreamer who wishes to train the subconscious mind in naturally being able to identify the in-between state.

After using the timer many times, you will soon realise that you have no need for it. You be able to bring on sleep paralysis on demand once you've adapted to the sensation. This is extremely effective and perfectly safe. You may feel a little sleep deprived the next day however, which is why we use this within the early hours of the morning, so that you still get the important deep sleep phase.

Method

Using the WBTB method. Wake up after five or six hours of sleep. Stay up for approximately twenty to forty-five minutes.

Turn on the timer (available as an MP3 or flash file that can be used on a MP3 player or computer)

Rest on your back or side. Make sure to leave one side of the headphones in the outside ear if you're lying on the side. To stimulate and compress the necessary energy or chakra points in the body, lay on the right side for males or the left side for females.

Fall asleep within twenty to thirty minutes. Just drift off to sleep and clear your mind. When you hear a beep, carry on and fall fast asleep. Remember to not move one muscle or twitch the face. This will become easier the more you try. If you do move, reset the timer and start from the beginning of the count again.

SGLD Techniques

The following methods are what I class as "SGLD Techniques." Through the years I have learned from my guide the best way to summon, maintain our bond's connection and psychically feeling my guide's presence and voice in waking and dream. I have worked closely with him, looking for a universal way for everyone to breakthrough and seek their guides. My hope is to share and inspire other dreamers to use these same methods and gain greater success. I would like to see more Spirit Guided Lucid Dreamers out there for the future. We can all learn so much from each other and from our sacred companions.

So what key methods can we use to strengthen and connect our relationship with our spirit guide?

SG Hand Mudra

My spirit guide has kindly given me a hand mudra that we can all use when initiating SGLD. When I have used this mudra, I have achieved lucidity every time and summoned my guide. The type of lucid dream has been very prophetic in nature.

I acquired this gift from the gods one magical night. I set my intention to gain new wisdom so that he could present to me a unique tool that will work for myself and others. After waking from an incredibly surreal astral projection experience, I found my hands positioned in a unique formation, one that I have never seen before. I got a great overwhelming sense that this was a gift from my guide and I would like to share it with you for the first time.

Obviously, there are no guarantees that this will work for you personally, as I have not yet tried and tested this on others. All I can offer are my experiences, along with the techniques that have worked well for me. What I experience and perceive may or may not be the same for others. But that doesn't mean that we shouldn't discover and experiment together. I hope this unique hand mudra from beyond brings you the same luck it has brought me.

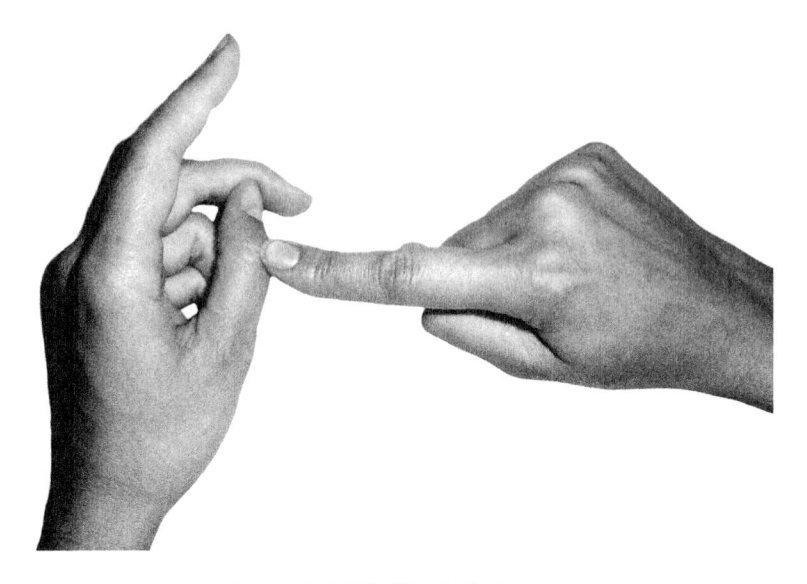

Figure 5 SGLD Hand Mudra

Method

At night when you go to bed, lay on your back, as this will be your main position. Do away with any itches upon your face and body and gently massage you temples and ears. Slightly stretch and tense all of your main muscle groups. Breathe deeply through your nose and into your belly, nice and slowly. Now exhale any unwanted worries and concerns, imagine them in the form of "grey impure smoke." When you breathe in, imagine a white and pure mist that brings you to deeper relaxation and serenity.

Now place both hands upon your upper abdomen. With the right hand, naturally create a pointing index finger with remaining fingers and thumb naturally being curled under. Using the index finger of the right hand, touch the thumb joint of the left hand, rest comfortably whilst still touching. Hands still positioned on upper abdomen. The tip of the left thumb now touches the first joint of the middle inside finger. Touch the inside, not the outer part of the middle finger joint to create a loop formation. Extend the left index finger outwards to form a pointing finger (don't be rigid, be relaxed). Let the ring finger and small finger now naturally curl under. Rest your completed hand mudra on the upper abdomen and don't be too flexed. Remember the aim is to fall asleep whilst holding this formation upon your upper abdomen, so be comfortable. As long as the points are in contact and you're relaxed, that's what's important here.

SGLD Meditation

We accomplish contact with our spirit family by consciously shifting our awareness within. Meditation is an ancient art that has been used for thousands of years. It's widely used across the globe. It connects us to places our linear minds cannot reach. It is the gateway to the infinite, a cosmic doorway to the universal source where all knowledge, wisdom and healing is within our grasp. Among countless other benefits, more significantly, it brings us closer to tranquil inner peace. Below is a simple, yet valuable, meditation one may utilise for SGLD.

Method

As you sit quietly and calm your mind, close your eyes and focus on the breath. We now recall our intention to meet our spirit guide family within our dreams. You may repeat a short mantra:

"I now attract my spirit family into my dreams."

Like all the phrases, say this mantra many times until you feel it set as a strong intention. Really believe in your words so that you can beam out your desire to the universe. Remember, we attract what we desire. You may now focus on your breathing again.

Ideal SGLD Time for Meditation

There is no right or wrong time to meditate, nor is there such a thing as a bad meditation. Anytime is a great time to meditate, how long you wish to do this is completely up to you. I do believe though, we should, if possible, start and end the day with meditation. Meditating just before and after sleep, will improve your general dreaming awareness substantially.

Below I share with you my ideal schedule, which I have found to be an asset in keeping my bond with my spirit guide vibrant. You will notice that I've added an extra awakening period during the middle of the night. I have found this to be helpful in strengthening my connection and benefits my clarity of mind. My ideal regime for meditating, starting with the evening practice, follows:

Meditate just before sleep (sitting upright in bed is fine) for thirty minutes or more

Lay back down to sleep on your back whilst holding the intention

Awaken naturally in the early hours of the morning (4 am preferably) and repeat meditation-recite mantra (sitting upright)

Lay back down and sleep on right side (for males) or left side (for females)

Upon awakening at a natural wake up time, meditate in bed (sitting upright) for at least thirty minutes

If you wish, meditate in the afternoon to further your practice even more.

SGLD Ritual

Another great aid to build up your union with spirit is to perform simple rituals focused on your guide, showing appreciation and loyalty. I do not claim to be a sorcerer of ritual magic nor practice regularly any sort of incantations. I believe in metaphysical science and the energies of the universe. I realise that this may be too "out-there" for some to comprehend, but before I tried this, I had never heard of a ritual. I performed the SGLD ritual for the first time in India one sunny afternoon and realised that among other things, it showed my utter appreciation and gratitude for all of my guide's wonderful teachings. This is so very needed. From then on, my dream studies began to really flourish; my dreams began to develop more meaning, deepening my consciousness even further.

People across the world have been performing rituals for thousands of years. In the western world today, however, it is more commonly known as something that's too holistic or even pagan. Even so, we have nothing to fear about the practice of a "ritual."

The truth is, when dedicating a small ritual to our guides to show appreciation, you do not need to acquire a certain spell book, be part of any cult, wear special robes or know how to speak in tongues! To make this work best, all you need is a little private time where you know you won't be disturbed, respect for your dream studies, some wild sage, a white candle, your dream journal, any crystals or special stones (if you have some) and a small table.

Method

First, turn off any mobile phones and unplug the telephone, lock doors if necessary so you won't be disturbed. Situate your items neatly onto the small table, light the white candle and sit comfortably, preferably on the floor.

Have your dream journal facing you and closed. Whilst sitting with hands clasped, begin to stare at your journal and connect to its radiant energy. Do this for five to ten minutes until you feel that all external thoughts are gone.

Now light the wild sage, and blow out the flame so it smolders. Let the scent circulate around your table by moving it around. Hold the sage over your journal for a brief moment and connect.

Now whilst holding the sage, say the following mantra;

'I call upon my highest self to guide me into the dream world. Please, spirit guide, connect with me now and light the way; I am ready for your next teachings…'

Repeat this intention over and over until you feel that it's firmly been set.

Place down the sage. Place your hands together with palms touching like you're praying, and place them over the heart.

Close your eyes, and bask in the moment with your guide. Say, thank you.

Meditate longer if you wish to.

SGLD Garden

Incubating and planting a dream seed into your subconscious mind is a great visualisation technique that can take you straight to your guide when deployed correctly. Similar to the MILD technique created by Stephen LaBerge, you first focus on intent, then conjure up a dream area of your choice to meet your guide. You can use a self-guided meditation audio file for this method or you can memorise it. By using this type of visualisation, you can gain a perspective of how it would look and feel, if you were to meet your guide in your lucid dream. The more you can imagine how it will be, the more likely you are to seal the bond. After you have practiced this before you sleep, you will have set the tone for your night's dreaming. Your guide will understand and start to hone in now that you wish to meet them consciously through dreaming.

Method

At night when you go to bed, lay on your back. Do away with any itches upon your face and body and gently massage your temples and ears. Slightly stretch and tense all the main muscle groups. Breathe deeply through your nose and into your belly nice and slow. Now exhale any unwanted worries and concerns, imagine them in the form of "gray impure smoke." When you breathe in, imagine a white and pure mist that brings you to deeper relaxation and serenity.

Imagine now that you are walking barefoot through a wonderful garden, the sun is shining and the sky is blue. This is your favourite garden, your very own spirit garden. Only you and your guide have access to its sacred grounds, so no one can disturb you.

As you walk barefoot along the soft grassy floor, you notice a beautiful white butterfly that is delicately fluttering past your vision. You feel relaxed and enchanted by its nature. You continue to follow it down the garden at a steady and soft pace. Along the way you decide to smell all of the wondrous aromas from the wild flowers. You breathe in through your nose and take in the flowers' scent, deeply and slowly you feel peaceful and tranquil.

You notice a big oak tree at the bottom of your garden and beneath this tree is a wooden bench. You decide to sit there to rest for a short while, relaxing and still breathing slowly and deeply. You can feel some of the fallen leaves beneath the soles of your feet. You smile to yourself and think how delightful your spirit garden actually is. No matter how many times you come here, it always leaves you highly fascinated with its ever-present beauty.

As you continue to look around your spirit garden, you start to feel your eyelids becoming very heavy, you try to keep them open, but it's too much for your tired eyes. So you happily give in and close your eyelids and you feel completely relaxed and content.

As you breathe slowly whilst contently smiling to yourself, you hear light footsteps in the distance along the grassy floor. The sound of someone treading on dry crunchy leaves carefully approaches you. You are curious about who it could be. As you remain calm and relaxed, you continue to leave your eyes shut and begin to trust your inner self.

The footsteps are sounding closer and closer to you, until they reach where you are sitting and then completely stop. You begin to sense a very familiar presence that's standing in front of you, and yet you don't think you know them. A very trusting energy emits from this mysterious character. A feeling of warmth from the sun surrounds your body and both you and this mysterious person bathe in its comforting light. The soles of your feet begin to feel warm and you feel deeply rooted to the earth.

With your eyes still closed, the figure in front of you sits next to you and delicately touches your hand. You feel the warmth of this soft and gentle hand. An ever-so-slight tingle shimmers across your skin. You can sense an abundant amount of love emanating from this caring grasp. You now hear a soft and gentle voice, "open your eyes." You slowly open your eyes to see who is sitting next to you. Your vision gradually comes into focus, to see, what you were always meant to see, your Spirit Guide.

SGLD Exchange Method

Having an out loud conversation with your guide, even if you've not managed to make direct contact yet, is a great way in offloading emotional concerns, doubts, ideas and solutions and generally keeps connection consistent. You can speak to your guide anytime you wish: in the car, on the way to work, at home—anywhere is fine! You can even talk telepathically when there are people around, though I do find I cover more ground when speaking aloud to my guide. This may seem that you're going crazy and your ego mind will wonder why you are talking to an invisible entity. There is no need to term this strange or weird, quite the contrary; it's one of the most natural modalities of the cosmos.

Speaking to our guides can really help us tie up any loose ends we have in our minds. As we all know, the mind can be very chatty at times, thousands upon thousands of thoughts are instantaneously formed everyday. When we are maintaining the bond, or even have that first time chat, it's important to understand that all our guides ever want is for us to offload what's on our mind. As a result, we can be expected to be free of any emotional misalignment. This is how spirit guides fulfill their galactic mission statement, by being there and supporting us, loving us unconditionally, anytime and anywhere. It is a two-way street, they help us and we help them. Above all, they wish to see us maintain a loving unity.

Making sure you don't get disturbed during the time of your exchange is also important. This is a very private and personal time between you and your guide. If you don't have access to a little alone time, I suggest taking a nice long walk in nature and speaking as you walk. It really helps clear your thoughts.

My own personal experience with this has been incredible and it is now deeply set into my practice. Yes, I felt a little silly when I first tried this. To an outside person, it would look like I was madly speaking to the walls of my bedroom! But, overtime, I realised the importance in speaking out loud to my guide. I just couldn't accept that the only time I could communicate with my guide was in my dream world. That would mean I would have to wait for over twelve hours in order to speak to him again! This was not enough for me, as I adore the guidance I receive! So, I began to miraculously speak out loud to him and I discovered that it strengthened our relationship.

Today, when I speak to my guide in waking reality, I feel that I'm working things out, and making more room for growth. He's a very good listener and I'm sure yours will be too.

As I speak to him, I can be sure that my guide is quietly taking down (non-physical) notes, planning out the next best thing for my consciousness. He influences my next dreams, sends me dream symbols and puts me in touch with the right people in waking reality. A spirit guide has infinite resources and love to give each of us. Similar to the intention we set in the SGLD ritual, speaking to our guides out loud and asking for the next teaching is also very effective. I've had many incredible journeys when I ask to be taught.

SGLD Summoning

When I first discovered my guide in lucid dreaming, I knew that my dream studies had suddenly taken a HUGE jump to the next level and into the great unknown. From then on, I made it my goal to maintain my relationship with my guide and show great respect as much as possible.

When you become lucid and fully grounded, you must seek out to find your guide. Chances are the guide will be close and waiting for your next move. It's really that simple, just ask out loud and be open to what will occur.

Method

Before you sleep at night, make sure to set your intention to become lucid in your dreams and to search for your spirit guide. You may use a mantra like, "I am now lucid and find my spirit guide." This should be repeated many times until firmly set into your mind. Twenty to thirty minutes of intention setting is a good amount of time.

You then become lucid in your dream. After grounding yourself firmly into the dream world (using the sacred steps), look around you and remember your intention to discover your spirit guide. Don't get too excited about this; breathe slowly and deeply and keep steadily moving. (Rubbing your hands whilst moving will also help you.)

Now find a spot you feel okay to yell in, and shout the following;

"Spirit Guide, Spirit Guide, Spirit Guide, It's me! Please show yourself!"

Now, continue to be patient, rub your hands together, remain calm and observe.

Suddenly, your spirit guide will show up somehow. If they were acting as a nearby character in your dream, they will reveal themselves to you, otherwise they can appear out of nowhere.

Depending on how lucid you are in that dream, you can telepathically pick up traces of your guide's presence. This could come as a shock if you're not used to the sensation. When you are consciously in their presence, you seem to have a deeper awareness and it feels like you've known them for an entire millennium!

You must believe and be persistent if they don't appear instantly. As mentioned before you may ask three times if you wish. I however did not need to. Since I made the connection, I have been working closely with my guide and I trust him implicitly. This can also apply for you, if the three-question rule doesn't bring you much luck, then try to gather a name you can use to beckon the spirit. The next time you are lucid in your dream, call out the name you received and see where this spirit takes you. I believe in synchronicity, so eventually, if not already, you will be certain to locate your own guide. Overtime you will see what teachings that spirit has brought you and know how loyal they are.

SGLD Awakening Method

Through intent, and exchanging thoughts to our spirit guides, we can be sure to achieve just about anything we desire. One experiment that turned out successful for me, which became one of my regular SGLD methods, was asking my guide to trigger my lucidity when I was unaware that I was in a dream. This happened many times. When I first tried this, I laid into bed, closed my eyes, then asked my guide to summon himself and trigger me into lucidity within the dream.

That very night, I had a vivid dream only to find a strange man shaking my arm whilst cutting through the dream's hypnotising storyboard, firmly alerting me, saying, "Nick, Nick, you're in a dream! It's me, your spirit guide!" I then became lucid and thanked him for helping to awaken me from my dazed-dream-walking. From there, we share a fantastic SGLD experience together.

This method can manifest in different forms, it will be interesting to discover what results other different dreamers experience. With success, this will solidify your in-dream skill, whilst helping you perfect the rate of your own lucid trigger. This has proved to be a great practice and solid method for future dreams.

Polyphasic Sleep & Dream

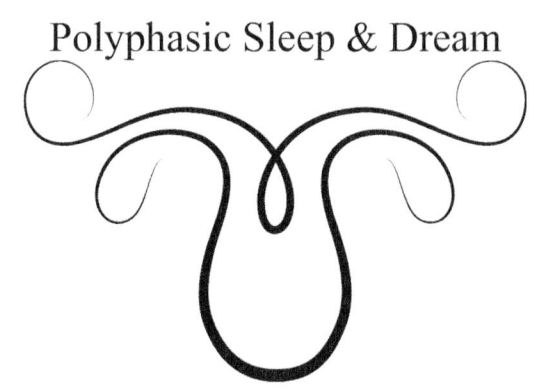

Chapter Six

When we rest our head to sleep at night, it tends to be for an average of eight hours. This time within a lifespan equates to an approximate of twenty-five years. That's almost a third of our lives that we are asleep, unconsciously dream walking. A large chunk of our lives is spent sleeping unwisely. This seems a little ludicrous when you look at the grand scale of things. Would you not like to add twenty-five to thirty years to your life? I know I would! When we consciously dream, we begin to extend our lives even more and still feel refreshed when we awaken. The Tibetan Dream Yogis refer to conscious dreaming as living two lifetimes.

We can also shorten the length of our sleep times, dream deeply and still feel refreshed. When we are born, we are naturally polyphasic sleepers. As a baby we wake and sleep multiple times a day. Nap times are generally short in duration. As we grow into a young child however, because of today's working system, we become monophasic sleepers (six to eight hours sleep, continuously with no naps in the day).

Our ancient ancestors knew about sleeping polyphasically and kept this unique sleep cycle for generations to come. Maybe they felt compelled to respect how nature originally intended it? If so, then somewhere along the line of history, this knowledge got lost, but was surely not completely forgotten.

In the 10th Century (AD), ancient Chinese texts, speak of a saint, named Chen Tuan. Among many things, he was mainly considered a master of inner alchemy meditation and therefore claimed the role of an archetypal Taoist mystic and immortal. Throughout ancient history, he shared many unique sleep-exercises. It is clear that he had a passion, for discovering perfected sleep and dream. Many of his apprentices would have to wait outside his front door before entering, so he could take his small, yet ever-so-important nap. The question remains, did Chen Tuan have a polyphasic sleep schedule? Did he discover a particular sleep cycle that promoted his lucid dreaming? Did this contribute towards his spiritual development?

Sure, the different sleep phases we all experience over the course of a night, have their vital use. Among many others, growth hormones are released to repair any cellular damage and serotonin levels are replenished in the brain. If we didn't sleep at all for five to seven days, we would be prone to hallucinations, mental instability and extreme brain fog. Evidently, sleep and rest is very important for the mind and body.

But, what if I could tell you that there was an incredible tool you can use to simply hack your brain and body to almost cheat sleep completely, be awake for almost twenty-four hours a day, and oh yeah, I almost forgot, still be at optimal levels and feeling great? You would probably say, yes! Many people today complain, "I have no time, I have a full time job, I need to have my eight hours of sleep or I will suffer," etc. These are all excuses, and not very good ones either!

The truth is, it's a myth that our bodies need the full eight hours or so. The good news is, that there is other sleep cycles available that may serve us more optimally. Many researchers and scientists have developed tests that study the success of alternate sleep cycles. How does the body react? What is the optimal sleep schedule? How is the mood stability of the subject? Is the brain running at optimal levels? How does is it effect our dreaming? These questions are just some of the important factors that are taken into account when researching sleep cycles.

Generally, the most common cycle in sleep today is monophasic. "mono," referring to one core sleep, consisting an average of six to eight hours with no naps until you go to bed again at night. If you slept from a biphasic cycle, you would have a core sleep of five to six hours at night and then be expected to nap around noon for ninety minutes. The nap in the afternoon is what most Europeans refer to as siesta. Polyphasic sleep cycles require a number of equally spaced naps throughout the night/day and sometimes a short core sleep if need be.

Sleep Cycles

Here a list of the five known sleep cycles available along with their pros and cons:

Monophasic. The more commonly used cycle. Six-eight hours of core sleep with no naps in between.

Pros: Easy to achieve because most people used this cycle since childhood, traditionally used today.

Cons: Feeling groggy at times, mild brain fog, feeling lethargic, aching muscles in lower back and neck. The Brains optimisation is not being fully restored and is not utilising its fullest potential.

Biphasic. Sleeping a core sleep of five to six hours and napping in the afternoon for ninety minutes.

Pros: Extremely easy to adapt to. Little or even no adaptation issues if you're already accustomed to a siesta. You feel generally more on top of things, your mood and focus is elevated. An added few hours to your routine can really go a long way.

Cons: Small inconvenience adjusting at the start. May feel slightly sleep deprived if used to the familiar eight-hour sleep. All in all, very minimal adaptation period.

Everyman. A core sleep that may consist of three hours or more, alongside multiple twenty-to-thirty-minute, equally spaced naps. Three to four naps can be used, equally spaced. Usually, six hours after the core sleep and four hours between each of the naps. This is very popular for many people who would like to ease themselves into a polyphasic cycle and then progress to another cycle to shorten their sleep time, like the Uberman cycle. Every short nap you take will trick your brain to fall directly into dreaming, almost instantly!

Pros: Much easier to adapt to than the Uberman/Dymaxion cycles. Dreams become incredibly vivid and much easier to remember. Some spontaneous lucid dreams too. Loads of wonderful time to work on your projects.

Cons: Much harder to adapt compared to a Biphasic schedule. Can take up to six weeks to feel settled into your new cycle. Sleep deprivation is noticeable for the first two weeks or so. Staying up in the night may feel strangely alien at first. Naps need to be taken at the allocated schedule, and you need to stick to it for the first month or so whilst the body adapts. If naps are altered during this time, or from oversleeping, then you will have to reset your body clock again and start over.

Uberman. This cycle significantly raises your chances in becoming spontaneously lucid during your dreams. The Uberman cycle consists of taking twenty-to-thirty-minute naps every four hours around the clock and sleeping a total of two hours. That's it! Many report experiencing high-level lucid dreams from day three onwards—in almost in every nap they take. That's potentially six lucid dreams per day!

Pros: Have ample time to complete all your projects. Lucid dream almost in every nap you take. Adaptation period is shorter than the Everyman cycle, lasting approximately a week or so. Like all polyphasic cycles, you will feel energetic and high-spirited once you finally adapt.

Cons: Naps must be taken, without fail, at the designated time. Otherwise you will risk all of your hard efforts and need to start over again. Time distortion can mess with your head a little, not knowing what day and date it is can be difficult to ascertain. Not having enough projects or duties can be boring with all this time available. The adaptation period is incredibly challenging for the first four days or so.

Dymaxion. Naptimes consist of thirty minutes long and taken four times in a twenty-four hour period. This total amount of sleep, similar to Uberman, is two hours. Only a few have successfully adapted to Dymaxion because of its very demanding nature. This does not mean it's not impossible, though. You can still achieve optimal levels with just enough sleep, in this case, two hours seems to be the most minimal amount. Adaptation time is approximately one/two weeks.

Pros: Less frequency of naps, so this gives you more flexibility when coordinating your days both professionally and socially. ahhh, time glorious time! Feel great and be at optimal concentration.

Cons: Very demanding adapting to the sleep deprivation during the early stages. People may wish to nap more frequently than every six hours. Risk of being slightly bored, especially at night, unless you have projects you can be working on to keep your mind stimulated.

Adaptation Period

Altering your standard cycle to a different one, can be a shock to the system. When transitioning to an alternate sleep cycle, you will experience a fair degree of sleep deprivation. The particular cycle you choose will determine how long the sleep deprivation will continue. During this time of change, make sure to eat as clean as possible. Successful polyphaser, Steve Pavlina, successfully adapted to an Uberman schedule for five and a half months. On Steve's blog, he has documented his Uber-journey and is a great read. Interestingly, he adapted very well and in only a short period of time, roughly about one week. He almost bypassed the dreaded sleep deprivation completely it seemed! He claims that this was most probably because of the vegan diet that he had already included into his lifestyle. No fried foods, caffeinated or alcoholic drinks were consumed either, which was an important factor. Helping our bodies by eating clean as possible will assist in a smooth adaptation period.

To get past the sleep deprivation stage, it is essential that our bodies achieve the REM (Rapid Eye Movement) sleep stage. When this occurs, we usually dream and can be lucid as well. When we train our bodies to be polyphasic, the early deep stage still needs to catch up. Which is why for the first week or more when adapting, we will not dream and our sleep will feel deep and groggy. It's just the body's way of catching up. Once it adapts however, and the more we take our short naps, the body will crave the stage four REM period (dream-time), which we all dearly love and need. Many report, that after getting over the sleep-dep-hump and experience their first polyphasic REM sleep, they awaken feeling completely rested and content. All from just taking a twenty minute nap!

Time Distortion

As we adjust our sleep pattern, our perception of time can seem to radically alter. Obviously the more hours we are awake, the longer it will be. But time starts to bend and twist all around us. Having a twenty-minute nap may seem small to someone who has never experienced being polyphasic, but this simply isn't so. How long it feels may be different from other cycles. I recall testing out an everyman cycle consisting of:

> **5 am – 8 am (3 hour core sleep)**
>
> **5 pm (20 min nap)**
>
> **11 pm (20 min nap)**

My well-deserved naptime seemed to last an entire millennia! Sometimes I'd wake up naturally after eighteen minutes or so, only to find some time still left on the clock. I couldn't believe my eyes. I was incredibly thrilled by this! Time as I knew it began to break down around me. Seeing the sunrise and set was my only linear buffer in understanding what day it was. Having, what felt like the ability to manipulate time, made me feel almost immortal. I suspect that a person who wishes to include an uberman schedule, time may distort even more. For me, I don't wish to try uberman just yet, though I probably will in the future. Today, I'm experimenting with alternate cycles, including the everyman cycle. But still feel that there may be an optimal way in altering these specific times to promote my lucid dreaming even more.

My Experience

My journey into lucid dreaming led me to experiment with my sleeping pattern. I was fascinated that it can have a huge impact on dreaming, just by staying awake longer than usual. I thought to myself, as long as I did my research on the subject matter first, everything should be fine. The more I researched successful polyphasers, the more I wanted to do it! I discovered many out there that had tried it. Some managed to make it work and even for a few years of their life, others unfortunately, including myself, gave in after a week or so.

I gave into the "sleep-dep monster," plain and simple—the number one ingredient that's not to everyone's palette I'm sure! We all like sleeping at night—who doesn't? But during the start of this process, you will find yourself more vulnerable than usual and will be extremely challenged. When you are tired, your brain instinctively takes over and tries and persuade you to just give in and go back into your original schedule.

You may have an internal battle, wondering whether or not to rest your head, even if it's just for a minute or so! One word, if this comes up, DON'T! Truth is, if you do, you won't get back up, so don't even take the chance. You may be the most headstrong person out there, but if you're not prepared to monitor this, you will be destined to fail. I like to instantly get up and take a quick walk outside if this occurs, or maybe splash some cold water on my face.

I wasn't disciplined enough with my good diet unfortunately. Although I knew eating as clean as possible, i.e. fruits and vegetables, was important, I did give in sometimes to things like breads and fatty foods. My awareness suffered slightly because of how sleep deprived I was. Saying that though, my girlfriend and I were on the road travelling, too. We were camping and driving really long distances. So my nap times were jolted out of their allocated slot.

This explains why many of these polyphasic web sites, clearly repeat the importance of preparation, especially during the adaptation period. They can't stress this enough and we shouldn't take this lightly. We must choose a planned period of time that we know our schedule won't be disrupted to cancel out all of our efforts. If we are to succeed, we need to make it as smooth and easy for ourselves as possible. We are most vulnerable to give in during the adaptation process and thereafter it will become far easier. Every sleep cycle has its own individual lengths of time for adapting; they can all vary from a week to a month or so.

Throughout the beginning stages of my sleep experiment, I didn't have any dreams. This lasted for about a week and was surreal for me. I was incredibly tired and really wanted the REM sleep stage to occur during my nap times so that I could feel refreshed again!

My goal was to adapt long term and to generally test the impact being polyphasic had on my lucid dreams. On the day when I slept longer than I should have done, I had the most profound SGLD experience! Most probably because I'd managed to build up the precious REM stages from previous days, thus resulting in a colossal rebound effect.

That night, I was catapulted into an astral projection, feeling strong vibrations, ascending to such a high degree of consciousness. My lucid clarity was something of a new nature that I can safely admit, I have only experienced a handful of times. Of course I've had countless lucid dream experiences, but the difference on that occasion was that I felt as though it was a temporarily transportation of my soul. Where we perceive we go to when we're lucid can feel like a vivid experience, but to actually soul travel to these places, to really transport to these foreign worlds and return back home safely, is an entirely different thing. No longer can it be deemed as a very profound dream; there is simply no comparison.

I saw my guide in a whole new light. I could see the very pores in his face, the gleaming iris in his eyes. The detail was more real than real. My emotional psychic senses were extremely enhanced. Telepathically communicating seemed only normal in this realm.

I woke up the next morning, not feeling guilty at all that I slept in. I confirmed my short experience into being slightly polyphasic as a great success! I now had the proof, that if I diligently stuck to a schedule and got through the adaptation period correctly, my lucid dreams would flourish even more. A whole new level of dreaming was now at my fingertips. I could possibly have multiple lucid dreams everyday. This obviously appealed to me, as I could spend more dream-time with my guide! I had always read that it improved lucid dreaming, but never had the experience, until now. This gave me the courage and push to give it another try. To see what other cycles out there that could work. I would be silly not to right?

Reset and Prepare

In the event of not being able to continue with the adaptation process, it is important to note, that we will need at least a few weeks to a month of recuperation with our previous sleep pattern if we are to try again. This will ensure that all bodily clock functionality becomes reset and a healthy platform is created for future tries. Otherwise, immediately going ahead after a failed attempt will only impede your progress into a vicious circle of trying new sleep schedules and failing. It seems to be a worthy practice when we use the art of patience, this included here will soon pay off. Be focused and don't give in to the sleep-dep monster!

A Helping Hand In Times of Need

Chapter Seven

As we become more evolved with our practice, we can be challenged with lucid/non lucid nightmares. With concerns and day-to-day stress we all experience, nightmares and disturbing dreams are likely to occur when we sleep. That's why it's important to really get to the heart of what's causing them instead of choosing to ignore it.

Nightmares can actually be a great way to establish what's happening in your waking life. Feelings of anger, stress, guilt and shame all contribute toward creating vivid, unsettling dreams. Reoccurring visits to a familiar place when you dream is a way of the subconscious mind signaling for you to pay close attention and take heed. Maybe it's a family home from where you grew up as a child, where most of your main childhood memories were formed? Maybe a life-changing event occurred for you in this very house, which you've now consciously chosen to block out and keep buried. Unsettled grievances can also appear in the form of a person/projection. Does this particular person ignite any unresolved issues deep within you? What memories do you have about this particular someone?

As humans, we are all instinctually programmed to survive when we feel threatened or in danger. It is deeply routed into our genetic makeup. When we have a nightmare our minds are going through such disharmony, showing us images and sensations that can give us quite a scare, just as if it was really happening. The most common thing to do would be to run away, which is a dream symbol for possibly avoiding (running away from) an emotional situation. Or, alternatively we'll try to fight back, only to find our clenched fists feel like heavy lead weights and everything is in slow motion.

The nightmare can go two ways from here, either we try to wake ourselves up within the dream just at the right time, or the monster or thing captures us and wins. We suddenly wake up with night sweats pouring down our faces, heavily panting and our hearts pounding like a drum. Our physical bodies really feel and believe what it experiences, no matter if it's in waking or the dream reality. To the body there is no difference. All of the physical reactions are there, just as if there was a threatening demonic adversary actually challenging us. It is only when we awaken from the nightmare, that we have a great sense of relief and comfort, returning safely back into our cosy warm beds.

Did you know that when we have an unsettling dream or nightmare, naturally commanding ourselves to awaken at the right time, this is classed as a form of basic lucidity? You may think you have never achieved lucid dreaming before, but that may not be the case if you have the ability to wake yourself up from a scary nightmare. You are already in the driver's seat heading towards conscious dreaming. Perhaps in a dream you may be plummeting at an incredible rate from a staggering high skyscraper and nano-seconds before you nearly hit the hard concrete floor, you direct your consciousness to wake up. This is being consciously aware within the dreaming mind. When we are put at risk or placed in a form of danger, our survival instincts kick in and take control, not the dream controlling us.

Facing Your Inner Demons

Learning to lucid dream is a fantastic way to confront those past demons and unresolved memories that our conscious minds would rather lay to rest. We can all learn so much from the other side of the coin if we wish to. Within every dark there is light and with every light there is dark. It is the universal system of opposite polarities and it is there to assist us gain greater consciousness. So harness those unsettling dreams and learn to recycle them; decode them and grow even more.

This mission, should you choose to accept it, will take great courage, but in the end, you will show your demons who is really the boss!

You've probably guessed by now that by requesting a particular intention to your guide (no matter how weird and wonderful), you will receive the thing you so intentionally desire. Which could even mean a dark challenge, if that is what you're setting yourself up for. To be put quite bluntly, if you are actually ready to confront these demons once and for all, then by all means, ask your spirit guide and it will materialise in front of your eyes within your next lucid adventure.

You may be thinking by this point, "Why would I put myself through so much stress and fear?" Well, the good thing is, that you're prepared more than ever now! I'm hoping you and your guide have finally connected to each other, and had many wonderful lucid adventures together. Your guide, throughout any of your adventures, is not only to help you along the way, but to protect you as well. Look at your guide as a galactic bodyguard if it helps!

If you feel curious to awaken that deeper part of yourself, to expand and grow even more, to never feel fear again, to experience immortality--that nothing can ever harm you again, I suggest confronting those demons within. It will benefit you with extra confidence and you will discover a newfound freedom. You will also undergo a magnificent inner healing and will finally be a master of your emotions.

SGLN Method (Spirit Guided Lucid Nightmare)

As you lay in bed at night to go to sleep, ask from your spirit guide; "Please send me a lucid dream, so that I can confront my inner-demons, please guide and protect me, thank you." Repeat this until you feel it is deeply routed into your mind, like with all the mantras from the methods. Request this with belief and emotion; we are not asking just words here. The words and letters themselves formulate a distinctive vibration corresponding with the intention in mind. So, be sure to place a feeling of strong desire behind your intention when repeating the phrase. Have courage and trust in your guide to deliver. Now, calm the mind and drift off to sleep.

The Crow People- SGLN Experience

Below is a Spirit Guided Lucid Nightmare entry from my dream journal. I would like to share it with you.

I am swirling in a wormhole with my guide. He is next to me and not touching. I must be getting the hang of this! There is a feeling of needles prickling my body in many places, it's slightly uncomfortable. It's similar to acupuncture! I seem to be transitioning somewhere. I can't see anything and it feels as though I'm traveling faster than the speed of light. The sound of a thousand crows surrounds me. I feel safe that my guide is with me, I ask telepathically if he can look after me if anything goes wrong. I immediately receive the feeling of security from him. The sensations of movement are beginning to slow down.

We stop; I open my eyes, arriving next to a beautiful crystal water lake. I'm standing on a wooden deck platform, my guide next to me. We walk to the center of the nearby village that seems to be towards the end of the wooden decking. There's a very colourful alien funfair happening! Big red balloons, children on mechanical rides laughing and screaming. I accidently bump into an old lady with a grey hood. I can't see her face, as it is shadowed. She speaks in a strange language. A dialect I have never heard before. She sounds slightly distressed, why is she venting on me, I think to myself.

I ask Clifftoft, "Why is she like this? Is she a projection?"

He turns round to face me and says with a slight smirk, "Projection?"

So she is a spirit then, I conclude to myself.

The old woman is still talking frantically at me, with the strange sounds coming out of her mouth. What message is she trying to give me? Could she be a witch? I think to myself.

I feel a huge surge of paranoia and uncertainty creep over me. The colours and vibrancy of the dream begins to fluctuate and flicker. I stand and observe the entire funfair and the people in it as they transform and degrade. The vibration is being lowered dramatically and fast. Lowered by who or what though? Could it be my uneasiness that is causing this to happen? Perhaps a knock-on effect of my uncertainty from the eerie old lady?

Then, to my horror, flying shadow-eagles, the size of a small minivan, pervade and dart across the night sky, screeching their deathly squawk with ear-piercing volume. I can't see my guide anymore. I fear I'm alone.

Now my vision is black and everything is completely silent. I feel a soft hand upon mine. I seem to be falling again, but I'm not able to see or hear. I feel a sensation of vertigo as I descend deeper and deeper into the unknown void, whilst clutching on tightly to my guides hands. It is all I have.

I hit the ground, and appear to be in a fiery cave. Walls aflame, narrow stone walkways that look too unstable to stand upon. Deep chasms of golden fire roar from the ground up. This is most certainly my hell! I feel absolutely petrified! For some reason though, I have my earth partner with me, so it's not all bad, even if she is a projection that my subconscious mind has created!

To my dismay, I notice in the far distance, on the other side of the fiery pit, a twenty-foot-tall beast. It stands like a giant, slender man from the waist down, and the upper half—head, neck and shoulders—is of a bird, like a crow. They look rather intimidating, "I really hope I don't run into one. Better keep my distance," I think to myself. I continue to walk down the unstable path whilst keeping my head down, only to find one of the tall beasts walking straight towards me with long strides. There're incredibly tall, and so much more when you are closer to them.

I keep my head down, and glance to see if he notices me. He doesn't, and his tall spindly legs thud passes me. But then to my horror, just as I'm about to reach the safe zone in completely passing him, I accidently touch his right leg! I suddenly hear a bellowing bird-like screech from above, his head immediately jolts to see what was beneath! I scream, arrhhhhh!!! Now I'm running as fast as I can (as if I were in the 100-meter sprint for the Olympics). The crow-man is chasing me down the narrow path at top speed. I shout for help from my guide, "CLIFFTOFT! HELP ME!" All of a sudden I see a colorful big chest with lots of yellows and reds in the distance. It appears to also have a heart emblem on its lid. Clifftoft has placed it there! I think to myself, "Yes, I'm saved!"

As my partner and I reach the large chest, the lid suddenly pops open. I look behind me and can now see the giant crow-man getting closer and closer. I return to look back at the chest, and hear Clifftoft's voice coming from deep inside it. He shouts, "Geeeeeeeet Innnnnnnnnn Nooooow!"

Without any hesitation, we both jump in. She gets in first, then me. We fall headfirst into a dark abyss of nothingness into the bottomless chest. As I descend I feel the crow-mans razor sharp claws touch the soles of my feet. But he was too late, as I was already long gone into the vortex. Thankfully because of my guide being there to help me. I wake up in reality with a great sense of relief. A deep sigh of relief leaves my lungs and I thank my spirit guide for lending a helping hand in that desperate time of need.

Upon Reflection

In understanding this SGLN experience, I felt an inner sense of achievement. I escaped the sinister clutches of the deathly crow people (as I like to refer to them), thankfully, because of my guide leaving me a heart-sealed escape chest to climb into! At the time of experiencing this SGLN, I was also in a fearful place in my waking reality. Like most of us, I panicked and felt trapped. The only thing that made sense to me was to look for the answers within my dreams and ask for my guide's help.

I have listed below the two major manifestations that stood out for me during my SGLN along with the questions that arose. Not all of these questions can be truly answered though, I believe it is how the dreamer individually perceives it, or more accurately, wants to perceive it. Not everything in dreams can be explained to serve our linear ways of judgment. Sometimes, future dreams can explain the hidden aspect of a past dream. There is no set formula in the timing in which we receive their distinct meanings. In the land of dreams, time yet again has no meaning.

Which is why having a spirit guide close at hand will always confirm to you, "the real hidden truth" of the mystical experience. The spirit never lies, and occasionally, the truth can hurt. They are not here with us to sugarcoat this information and meaning, so we must be mentally prepared for receiving it at any given time.

The Hooded Old Lady

From meeting her in the first realm, I noticed how direct she was when she approached me in a frantic manner. The question is, why she seemed distressed? Why did I hear, what sounded like, incantations under her breath? Was it a spell of some sort that transported me to the land of the crow-people? Did my sprit guide know her beforehand?

I believe I met her in dreams months after this SGLN, whilst also being accompanied by my spirit guide. She appeared many times, transitioning in and out, offering holistic guidance and advice to the spirit friends I was with.

I recall in one lucid dream,

The old lady and my spirit family are all seated around an oval wooden table, she wears her familiar dark robes and uses what appears to be tarot cards. She sits quietly as she carefully examines the cards. The other spirits, including my guide, are gathered around her sitting patiently. I sense telepathically some thought-based noise coming from them all, but unfortunately can't directly decode what is being asked.

But it is obvious to me that they are all communicating this way. Then something got the attention of the ambiance within the small gathering. I sit there, smaller than them, like a five-year-old child, amazed and innocent. The hooded lady raises her left hand and extends her index finger outwardly to point in front of her. The vibration and sensory atmosphere drastically changes, as the feeling of us all gasped in anticipation of what the old lady was going to do next. A swarming feeling overfills us all as she is about to deliver a prophetic answer to some lucky person.

I think to myself, whom is she going to point at? Her frail arm and finger gently moves over to her right side and points to me. I gaze upon her wrinkled and withered yet wise and effervescent features. She has kind eyes, which gives me the certification that she's genuinely a nice spirit. I receive a profound message through my mind's eye, silently asking me what I would like to know. "One question..."she asks.

Not thinking about what question to ask, I buckle under pressure because of the excitement. I ask her telepathically, "How is my progress with my ability to lucid dream & astral travel so far?"

She then replies, softly speaking, "You are good at your transitional exits."

Transitional exits, I think. Oh yeah! She is referring to how I can transition to other realms from within the dreamstate with great ease.

Originally, I found this particular method fairly challenging during the early stages of my lucid dream development and needed my guide to show me how to get to these places. In retrospect, after I received the wise old lady's words of encouragement, I began to be more independent of my guide's help in transitioning and progressed confidently. Hearing her say this gave me the added belief in myself to transition and perfect my skill even more. She said just the right thing, at the right time, to help me go to the next stage in my dream development.

She seems to be watching over me, observing in different dreams, whereby I recall seeing a shimmer of a hooded old lady. She either blends in with the background or walks past me quickly. I believe she is watching, here to help me if I ever need her. However, I don't think I'll get her to repeat the spell that could potentially send me back to the underworld anytime soon!

Tall Beats (Crow People)

At the start of the transition into this SGLN, my sight went dark and I heard what appeared to be, thousands of crows flying around my astral body. A 'Crow' is the symbol, for death and rebirth.

After the degradation of the dream, I then emerged in a place of fear and death. There, I encountered gigantic beasts with the appearance of the head of a bird and the body of a man, as they walk along fiery pits of darkness. It was very menacing and all too frightening. Was this my hell? Was this an elaborate manifestation of my subconscious? Why would I be sent here at this time? What is the lesson I am to learn, other than feeling absolutely petrified!

I feel that my guide's key message throughout this SGLN was the following:

"Even in the place of pure darkness, there will always be the opportunity to escape and transcend it at will. That fear, can always be dissolved instantly where there is, love."

I decided to research the tall beasts. I later named them 'Crow People' in my dream journal. I discovered that ancient Egyptian mythology had beings with some shocking similarities to these creatures.

Figure 6 Horus, Egyption God

Horus the God of the sun and moon (See. fig.5) has been depicted throughout Egyptian history in many forms. Other documented records show that he was the god of the hawk or falcon—which explains the bird-like head that's depicted throughout ancient history.

I'm not claiming that what I experienced was the realm and home of such a god. Nor, am I declaring that their heads were conformed as that of an actual crow. However, the idiosyncratic similarities they share are striking. Before this time, I had never explored Egyptian mythology, so it seemed even more surreal that my subconscious could conjure up such a thing.

Almost a year later however, not having any more 'dream-house-visits' by the crow people, I encountered something that I cannot explain—even today. I haven't asked my guide to clarify this as I feel it's not the right time to do so. My partner and I visited a particular farm in France. Along the way, I see many hawks soaring high in the blue sky. I took it as a Mirrored Awakening as recent dreams had shown me that hawks are closely connected to me.

Many times, I noticed several of them flying beside our van, it almost seemed that a great force followed us. As I drive, I am thrilled by a sense of protection from them. I decide to check my digital wristwatch to confirm that it was a sign from my spirit guide. I was correct! Every time I saw a hawk(s) along the open road, the number eight appears suddenly on my watch and to the very second! (I speak of this in greater detail in the next chapter, 'Mirrored Awakenings'.)

We finally arrive at our destination all drained from the long trip, our friends greet and welcome us. They then notice something incredibly strange. They look up and start taking photos. I turn my head to see what it was they were all excited about. I look up and see fifteen to twenty hawkes all circling high above our heads! The lady we were staying with claims to have never seen so many in all her twenty years of living there! Nothing of this magnitude, that's for sure.

We were all shocked just how incredible and privileged this sight was. After all of the hawks we'd seen on the way there, we were still blown away by seeing the group of them upon arrival! Our friends continued to take photos, and later deemed it as an omen about our visit. We were privileged and a little confused at the same time. I wasn't sure what to believe. I felt connected to the majestic birds that appeared to have followed us to our destination.

The weirdness however didn't stop there. That night on the farm, my partner and I lay down to sleep for the night in our caravan. As I drift off, I feel sensations across my body, vibrations and extreme tingling up and down my spine. I hear whispery sounds surrounding me. I feel a little unsettled but decide to go with it and surrender. I call upon my guide for protection. My vision is completely black as I enter the dark void between wake and sleep. The whispery voice pervades my anxious curiosity. I telepathically engage with this mysterious voice, "Who are you?" I ask. The voice replies to me in a whispery and mystifying voice, "I, am, Horus..."

As I explained before, I cannot offer answers as to what actually happened here and why I encountered a voice that claimed to be named Horus. What's interesting to note however, is that before this experience, I didn't know the name at all. When I researched this name from ancient times I came across the Egyptian god, named Horus, who oddly resembled the hawk/man hybrid of my dream. Seeing all of those hawks circling above our heads that day, was said to be unheard of and possibly an omen. The chain of events that started a year earlier when I discovered the crow people SGLN, seemed to have been a build up for the 'Horus' dream I encountered.

I feel intuitively that Horus is not to be feared. I feel protected by him and although he is depicted to be part hawk, the presence of these animals, including eagles, comfort me still today.

Mirrored Awakenings

Chapter Eight

Summoning our spirit guides, once we've learned how to connect with them in our dreams, can almost become addictive. This shouldn't be a problem for your guide, as he will always be there watching over you and is ever grateful for your loyalty. By keeping regular contact, you will feel the presence of your guide's advice on a subconscious level. We reach this state by being completely open and receptive to the divine guidance. As you progress together in expanding your two-way consciousness, strange and synchronistic events will begin to crop up. The message is subtle to begin with, but the more you recognise and note each one, the more frequently they will start appear. You don't have to wait around twiddling your thumbs. You can start the process right now!

Take a small walk somewhere alone, be completely lucid and in the moment, (similar to the practice in the SGLD adaptation) and try noticing what's around you. Observe the people who walk past you? Do you see any numbers that seem odd to you? Can you hear music or any other sounds? Maybe the music and the lyrics you hear have some significant meaning to you?

We need to open ourselves up energetically to receive celestial guidance—this is the central message that I give to you. We start this journey by trusting our guides to show us what we sometimes miss or do not fully recognise.

You may already be receptive to these qualities, be more aware and know the feeling of your psychic awareness. If so, then congratulations. This will be a great foundation to build upon with your SGLD practice. Don't worry if you can't yet—trust and believe that the signs of your guides are always in motion, all we have to do is open our hearts and trust.

The signs which your guide will send you, can be a humorous thing in the spur of the moment. The feeling of an instant rush shoots through you as the adrenalin levels rise, the hairs on the back of your neck will stand on end. All logic has ceased to operate at this point unveiling the linear mask we all commonly wear. The message can appear anywhere and anytime.

When the bond is fully sealed between you and the spirit, you will have questions and concerns that need answering; a surprising psychic impulse then strikes through you, leaving you wondering how you ever felt such a thing to begin with. This can happen even when watching television or listening to the radio. They can happen anytime, there are no rules. The psychic sensations you are receiving comply with the extra-sensory capabilities that are in harmony with your higher self. Your guide is sending you instantaneous advice and guidance on a psychic level. We pickup on this and become attuned to its perceptible sensation. I personally call this phenomenon a Mirrored Awakening.

The definition of a Mirrored Awakening is the following:

'Two worlds reflecting each other symbolically in wake and dream, in a synchronistic nature between you and spirit.'

If you haven't already, monitor each time you sense a Mirrored Awakening, or something you feel is a message from your guide, no matter how un-real you perceive it to be. You can even use a small pad and write down what it was, the day and where, etc. This will give you a good reference at the start of your SGLD journey by building up your senses to notice the signs from spirit.

My Mirrored Awakening

A few years before I knew how to lucid dream, I discovered strange reoccurrences of the same number. The number 8. Many times I saw this number appear to me in public places, far too many times to deem it as a coincidence. I first began to notice the number in post offices. Whereby, I'd be queuing and waiting for a digital number to be called out from 1-10. Then when it came to my turn the number eight cashier desk would be announced. This happened to me every time!

If I were with family or friends in the postal queue, to make the waiting time more interesting, I'd play a funny game whereby we had to guess our designated number. Of course I chose correctly and the winning number was indeed eight. My friends and family were always astonished that I knew. I felt that this was obviously more than just luck. There must have been some bigger reason to all of this.

The more I showed my interest in number eight the number increased. Everywhere I went the number followed me and began to be a personal friend of mine. During card games, number plates I owned, public transport numbers, house numbers I lived in and membership numbers, generally glancing at the passing time, the list just goes on and on, and continues still today.

The Real Meaning of Number 8

As I progressed through the development with my guide, I got more curious to know the inner truth of number eight. Why this particular number? What did it actually mean? My partner was studying the ancient art of numerology at the time, so I was able to check the significance of the number eight.

I found that the number's most prominent, key meanings included: abundance, achievement, strength, self-disciplined, power, psychology, success, intensity, supervisor, provider and grandeur. I was thrilled to see this, as you can probably imagine. Every time I encountered an eight, I resonated with these words which gave me added encouragement. Every number-eight-awakening, showed up instantly from either a digital watch or any other clock-based timer I gazed upon. I felt empowered, strong and confident. I had moments of being spiritually self-assured about any challenging situation, knowing full well that I could execute any task I put my mind to.

Today, I have discovered many observations regarding my mirrored awakenings on number eight. Now, I notice something even more surreal—it now appears when my outlook and mood is calm and centered. When I'm happy and laughing, enjoying the moment, trusting, allowing, sharing, showing gratitude to all and having a perfect day. I cannot tell you enough, how many times number eight randomly appears to me! Single eights, double eights and triple eights, all appear precisely when I feel the essence of the mirrored awakening.

Of course it is easy to see numbers appear in the world today. Numbers are everywhere and play a huge part of our society. Look around you now; do you see any numbers? This turns out to be a decent arrangement for my guide and I, as I have infinite resources to check numerically. I now understand it is my guide approving how I am at that given time and what my thoughts are. It's a numerical divine guidance system that I can utilise anytime I wish. I'm constantly and consistently staying connected to my guide's essence through number eight, and improving my decision-based thinking because of it.

Reading the number eight can have positive or negative connotations depending on the situation or thought process at hand. For instance, if I were in a moment of weakness, about to engage in a heated disagreement with someone, I would glance down at my watch discreetly, or see another nearby number. If I'm feeling particularly intolerant that day, the number will most definitely show itself to me.

I read this as a sign from my guide, reminding me to have inner strength and forwardly act with the highest part of myself. I will now opt to swallow my pride and instead be good to others, not choosing fear and giving in to hate, being more open in understanding how the other person feels. Pride and anger vanish, giving me the secret ingredient for greater communication and inner peace. All because of this little magic number provided by my spirit guide.

My guide is forever watching over me, timing the number sequences just right, to help shape and guide my consciousness.

Even so, at the end of the day, we are presented not a test, but more accurately, an opportunity. There is always a choice before us. We are never forced into anything. This is an opportunity to choose this way or that way. Which-way you eventually decide upon, will be the one you were always meant to choose. Then more opportunities will appear, giving us a window of options that may or may not lead to inner growth, it's our call. Knowing how to transform negativity into positivity has helped me no end, making me second-guess within that moment, before I make a wrong judgment.

Of course, those of you out there who have made contact, you can ask your guide any questions in your mind. I made it one of my SGLD quests one day, to find out the true meaning of my number eight so that I could gain more insight to its mystery. I wanted to have my guide's view on this, to see if what I found out through numerology was in fact correct.

This was my SGLD experience after setting my intention that night, to gain wisdom on my sacred number:

I'm in a dark abandoned castle, fighting off vampiresses. There are three of them and they have very large spiky teeth. They are grabbing me with their gripping claws and are screaming to overcome me. Because of this traumatic moment, I'm now spontaneously lucid (DILD). My conscious self is in the driving seat and I confidently ask, "Why are you doing this?"

They don't stop; they continue their wickedness and ignore my questioning. I exit quickly by flying high up into the night sky. I soar higher and higher, I call upon my guide to assist me in overcoming this horror. I translocate away from the vampire women. I appear in a late-night bar. My guide is serving drinks to other spirits at the bar. I walk over and greet him. I thank him for pulling me out of the tight squeeze with the vampiresses.

I ask, "Can you tell me the real meaning for number eight?" He quickly pulls out an upright large glass box, almost as tall as me! He turns it around so that the other side is facing me. I notice a rope that's intertwined throughout the back panel and it forms a big number!

I say, "Hey that's an eight!"

My guide replies, "Yeah, it comes with instructions!"

After decoding my guide's message regarding the meaning of number eight, I understood that the rectangular case he showed me had significant symbolic meaning. The glass front suggests a separation of the two worlds that becomes clear when peering through it.

I believe glass, to be similar to the mirrored awakening definition I made earlier. The large case turned round and then behind it, the rope was what kept it all interwoven. The symbol for rope mainly means strength and power. (Rope can also mean other things depending on the context of the dream.) The number eight was depicted within the formation of the tie of the rope. This number was now a confirmation from my guide, it is a symbol for strength and power for me to use. I have access to this powerful source, any place and time.

Just when you least expect it!

One of the most explicit number eight experiences I've had, blew my mind out of the water! In my younger years, I was a musician and a close friend of mine kindly asked me to perform at a club in Switzerland. It was a superb venue, with lots of really fun people there, welcoming me and making sure the night went smoothly. I then had to go backstage where I met one of the music promoters. As he and I were talking, laughing enjoying the ambiance, I notice him carrying a single card from a deck. He held an eight of clubs.

I said, "Hey why do you have that?"

He replied, "Oh, this? It's my lucky number eight card! I take it everywhere I go."

To my surprise, I said, "That's funny! That's my lucky number too!"

He passed me the lucky card, and says, "Here hold this!" He took off his T-shirt, and shows me his upper torso, which was full of tattooed number eights! He was absolutely covered in them, small ones, big ones, on every arm all across the back and chest. You name it!

He said, "Number eight is my lucky number. It guides me throughout life! I don't know where I'd be without it!"

I got shivers all over me; I couldn't believe what I just witnessed! I immediately told him that I too have had the same guidance and odd occurrences with this number. To think that someone I've never met before, in a different country, had tattooed a number all over his body—that he feels has been guiding him throughout his entire life too! Now that is a Mirrored Awakening.

Finding your Metaphysical Key

Numbers was my key to notice my guide and what messages he wished to share. My number eight tool has really become more wonderful through the years. The number literally first showed itself with no real effort on my side. It led me to my lucid dreaming interest in many ways, shaping my thoughts to better myself, to think of my actions before an emotional imbalance was likely to occur and to look within myself for the answers I seek.

You may not need to use a number system like me. Of course, if this is what's already evident to you, then you must continue; go with it and search more of it. I don't know if this is a universal numerical rule that often happens to others, but I feel that the metaphysical key to your guide's messages will naturally raise its head when the time is right. When we're fully open and willing to surrender to the trusting forces that be, always keeping an open mind. It is my belief that only then, will we start to see these incredibly mystifying synchronicities that turn up in our lives.

Clifftoft Rock

Whilst travelling around Europe in early 2011, I recall having a SGLD that made me better understand the reflective nature of my Mirrored Awakenings. After I became lucid in a dream, I summoned my guide to be with me once again—he always appears to me in exactly eight seconds.

He stands in a quiet city park that's set in autumn time. All the dead dry leaves are golden brown lying on the grassy floor. We speak for a while, then after walking ahead of me, he beckons me over to a large rock. He kneels on the edge and I sit beneath looking up.

I talk to him about wanting to deepen my dream studies and to find a connection with the Taoist teachings I had been researching. He sheds light on the topic, energising me and inspiring me to go more with the flow—not to force any situation and to let events unfold naturally.

"Everything has its time" the spirit says.

I respected his caring words of wisdom, and woke with a newly refined viewpoint in how to proceed gently with no pressure and to be more in the now.

A few months later, my partner and I, travelled to the north of France where we stayed with some good friends of ours for a short time. It was a house that didn't have much space unfortunately. With two kids, two dogs and four adults, things seemed to be cramped. Thankfully, the surrounding forestry was incredibly rich with healing pine trees, luscious green fields, wild deer roaming freely and stunning horizons as far as the eye can see.

One day I went to clear my head and took an intuitive walk into the unknown.

I noticed a path that had trees on both sides and I stood upon brown crusty leaves. I intuitively felt my guide's presence as I walked slowly ahead. Something was different about this path, but what? I felt as though I've been here before! This all looked far too familiar to me.

After walking so far, climbing a few fences here and there, I came across a beautiful small brook. I carefully placed one foot in front of the other and crossed the stepping-stones to get to the other side. I then climbed this big hill not knowing what was at the top. There is not a person in sight or sound. Only the slight howling of the wind, shifting my balance from one place to the next.

When I reached the top of the hill, a great sense of achievement hit me. I felt free and amongst Mother Earth's beauty. I looked around my panoramic scope of the surrounding hills and felt a real sense of freedom. I walked along the top and see a large rock situated in the centre of the field (see fig.6). It is the only rock here? I thought to myself. What an odd place for a rock to be here.

As I approach this rock, a large sense of a mirrored awakening overcame me! I quickly check my digital watch to confirm that what I felt was correct. I am right. Yes! It's exactly, to the second, 3:48pm! This means that my guide is notifying me about this rock. I realised that it's exactly the same rock as the one I had in my SGLD experience with him a few months earlier.

For the next few months, my partner and I stayed in that area. I would always visit this rock and talk to my guide. It was a place where I could exchange my thoughts and let go of any doubts and concerns. I used the SGLD exchange method here many times; it was truly my personal sanctuary. I meditated at the rock most days, feeling the strong presence of my guide. It was such a secret and beautiful place.

My lucid dreams were not only a place for him and I to talk, but also a place where he would present clues for physical future events—on this occasion, the large rock. Just as we talked on the big rock in the lucid dream, we talked at the big rock in waking reality. This was another tremendous mirrored awakening for me. The picture below is the actual site where I visited regularly. I decided to name it, 'Clifftoft Rock'.

Figure 7 Clifftoft Rock

Conclusion

I hope that you have discovered and achieved something inside of you, that you may have never thought possible. By practicing the methods within this book and setting the right tone for the mind, your intention has been put into motion. You can enjoy the fruits of your galactic friendship and be forever guided through wake and sleep.

The three initial key elements for SGLD are, Intention, belief and practice. Once you fully comprehend these important factors, you will thrive towards maintaining the connection between you and spirit.

Infinite knowledge and wisdom is within us all, and the answer to access and unleash powerful ancient abilities is here and now. Here is a quote from the entrance to the College of Priests, Temple of Horus at Edfu, Egypt:

"Knowledge is the Way to Life;
The Way to Life leads to the Way to God.
The Way to God leads to Inner Knowledge.
Inner Knowledge leads to Wisdom.
Wisdom becomes Life."

We are all born with the metaphysical ability of conscious dreaming, among many other 'superhuman' qualities we may or may not be aware of. It is not something that we have to reach and strive for. More simply, it's a case of remembering our natural birthright, returning back home and communicating to the source once again, which is always listening.

Breaking free the chains of time is an important stance we take when unleashing the power of self and spirit. Third dimensional time, which we all experience, is merely an illusion. Yes, this is the structure for how we base things, defining our past, present and future. But, when we delve deeper into the inner-dream and transition regularly with our spirit guides, linear time seems to naturally break away.

No-more stress to take the kids to school when there're late! No more running down the escalators because you overslept again! Linear time seems secondary now and you can cheat its very structure through dreaming. As a result, the physical reality brings forth added synchronicity, so our lives become easier and more free-flowing. You will be more aligned with the universal energies. Life changing moments that will greatly bring happiness to you are now presented at certain events. Strange occurrences, unexplainable situations and meeting new acquaintances for the first time, all seem to fall into place just at the right time. The more we let three-dimensional time be the governor of the mansion, the more likely we will remain chained to the linear mindset and never exceed and remember our incredible divine nature. We can all be living and dreaming outside of the box.

'Control the mind, but never be a prisoner from the mind.'

Lucid dreaming and SGLD, pushes the boundaries outside of the parameter we live in and things miraculously start to appear, without our physical intervention. It is perfectly timed and perfectly aligned when we have our spirit selves by our sides.

Dreaming lucidly, not only for the fluid world we enter when we sleep, but exemplifying this through physical reality too, will break down this illusory wall completely. For it is only another type of dream; the principles between different dimensions are still present. Planet Earth is vibrating at a frequency that provides a solid structure from energy. As we go up the scale, simply put, solid matter becomes fluid and energy can be easily transformed.

Thoughts are also comprised of energy. So, when you set your intention to meet and be guided by your spirit helper, if you hold the meaning and repeat it like a mantra, the energy will be transformed into a reality. Anything is possible, there are no limits to what thought/energy can provide.

As a child, I always heard the biblical phrase, "Ask and you shall receive," which has a lot of resonance when viewing this perspective, irrespective of your belief system.

I believe we are already connecting with our guides, even before we are born and in many previous lives. It's only when we are born into the physical human form that we detach from the previous memories. Our memory is wiped clean and we start fresh into the unknown, and the cycle begins once again. It's up to us to reconnect to them once again, to make it our goal; if we are to receive help and guidance from a spiritual being to begin with, then we should be able to access it anytime we want. If we choose to receive it, then it shall appear. It is that simple. No complicated technique is needed. The most effective things tend to be the simplest things in life.

Keeping everything simple and fluid throughout all of our SGLD efforts, also in our waking life, is a wonderful basis on which to go forward.

The Taoist teachings put it beautifully, "Always be in harmony with the source that created you and that is love." My guide and I have enjoyed sharing the fruits of the Taoist teachings for many years. He incredibly orchestrates them to me in the dream world with profound symbolic communication and imagery, where there I'm offered opportunities for growth of my consciousness.

Flowing not forcing

Always flow down the stream with ease and comfort. Not upward and against the current, where you cannot find strength to paddle back up. If you suddenly veer off course and accidently hit the banks temporarily, then don't worry. It is a well-learnt lesson to avoid this next time. You then paddle back to the middle of the downward stream, where there is no confrontation and return to centering yourself once more. With comfort, with ease and with spirit.

I would like to take this opportunity to thank you, the reader, for allowing yourself to be open to other possibilities in dreaming. We can all learn so much from Spirit Guided Lucid Dreaming; we must be willing to discover a deeper part of ourselves. I feel as though in the time I have spent with my guide, he has given me a fast-track potent understanding of my spiritual makeup, emotions and fears. I do not know what my life would be like without him now I have found him. I imagine I'd feel quite alone and incomplete. I am incredibly blessed and grateful.

Even as I write this, I glance over at the clock, triple eights instantly appear, telling me that my guide is present and is showing me his appreciation to my kind respects. When we show our appreciation, it is heard and is immediately sent back with the mirror of love and guidance.

If we ever feel doubt towards our higher self, we should be aware, that we essentially doubt ourselves in the process. Within, we are already complete—we don't need someone or something to rescue us from a hole we may think and feel we're in. It is just a case of becoming aligned once again and remembering.

The help and guidance you seek is within you right now and has always been there, even as you're finishing this book! Your spirit guide is always present, and is internally within you, not outside of you. The spirit is you, and you will always be spirit. It is one and the same.

Guided lucidity and noticing the messages from beyond, simply reconnects the spirit part of us, consciously walking, one step at a time.

About the Author

Nick Barrett is the author of eBooks, 'Spirit Guided Lucid Dreaming' and the 'Dreamscape series one', along with being the blog author for the 'Alwayz Lucid' website and creator of fictitious cartoon character, 'Dr. Lucid.' Nick is also a trained Medical Qigong practitioner levels, 1-3.

Some mysterious force always guided the author's journey from when he was a child, what that 'force' was exactly, he wasn't sure! He then made it his prime objective to find out the answers through his lucid dreams and thusly, located and sealed the bond with his spirit guide. He confides in his guide regularly, in times of need, to access higher states of awareness and to seek new ancient wisdom. Throughout all that he writes and what is shared, his guide is forever by his side advising him along the way.

Nick now dedicates his full time, in sharing with others to help raise global consciousness, and provides insight into the true nature in spiritual companionship and lucid dreaming. Nick is also working on a children's book project for 5-9 year olds, which is aimed towards bringing more awareness to the art of *lucid dreaming* for future generations to come.

"When I dream, I will know I'm dreaming..."

Printed in Great Britain
by Amazon